Pride

Of The

Worm

Pride

Of The

Worm

Norm Sawyer

Cover Art by Kane Sawyer

ISBN: 1988226147
ISBN-13: 978-1988226149

Published by

First Page Solutions
Kelowna BC Canada

CONTENTS

FOREWORD

Every Friday morning at 7:00 AM, a small group of men sit down to breakfast at the local White Spot restaurant in Kelowna, British Columbia. It has been like this for many years, meeting and discussing life. No agendas, no boundaries.

Norm writes his blog during the week and posts it to the web very early Friday morning, so breakfast is ripe for a blog review. Many times, new topics and titles for the blog emerges during breakfast banter and, in time, a blog on a topic usually appears.

I have personally known Norm for over twenty-five years. My daughter and wife have both been taught by him when they attended Bible college. I have grown to trust his interpretation and insight into Scripture that seems so practical, yet pretty darn deep and often astounding.

Our connection goes back much further, though, almost forty-five years… when we both worked for the same firm, yet never encountered each other. Norm never left the firm, earning his way as an on-the-road salesman: a tough profession in the best of times. Throughout his career he faced challenges to his integrity and character but always seemed to come up on top. Integrity was - is- paramount in his life. The owner of the company referred to Norm as the company's pastor. Not far off.

Surprisingly, Norm grew up functionally illiterate, neither being able to read or write. Therefore, he found it difficult coping with everyday situations. He figures that it's God's sense of humour that led him to becoming a writer and teacher - that and a lot of hard work. He is pragmatic, a hard worker and a life-long learner. He is a pastor's teacher, not being afraid to say what is on his mind and heart. Most of all, he is trustworthy.

Norm is probably the most disciplined man I know, but not obsessive about it. He had a stroke that almost killed him a few years ago, and I watched as he acquired medical and nutritional knowledge that challenged his doctors to the point where the doctors were asking him for advice. I watched him lose seventy-five pounds and keep it off. I watched him as he regained his health through diet and daily exercise. I watched him as he wrestled with 'religion' and how to discard it for 'relationship', tearing up his worldly credentials in favor of just listening to God.

Norm's blog reflects life from a practical sense, but with a directed Godly purpose: insight into human character and more importantly, insight into God's character. He wrestles with God almost daily, an intensely personal quest that seeks answers that lead to wisdom and then to personal action.

Norm Sawyer is unique, as we all are, but somehow Norm is a bit more unique than the rest of us.

Robert Riker
Author "DOUBLING, A Guide for the

Professional Salesperson" (McGraw-Hill)
"SELLEGRITY, Doing the Right Thing – Regardless" (on Integrity and Ethics)

PART ONE
OVERCOMING

Walking along an old street I was reminded of the unknown areas we head toward to overcome our fears.

PRIDE OF THE WORM

Proverbs 16:18 Pride goes before destruction, and an haughty spirit before a fall.

There is an ugliness about pride and it can look so ugly that it has a stench to it. As my uncle with a strong French accent says, "Pride is hugglly." There is a pride, however, that is even uglier; it is the pride of the worm. This is a reverse pride that is always contrary to what God is saying about us. God says, "We are the righteousness of God through Christ." 2 Cor. 5:21 **For He made Him who knew no sin to be sin for us, that we might become the righteousness of God in Him.** The reverse pride says, "Oh no, I'm just a sinner saved by grace." God says, "He loves us as equally as he loves Jesus." John 17:23 **I in them, and thou in me, that they may be made perfect in one; and that the world may know that thou hast sent me, and hast loved them, as thou hast loved me.** Reverse pride says, "Oh no, how could God love a person like me?" and so on and so on. These people beat themselves up and bring themselves down and are harder on themselves than God is, all in the name of trying to be humble. In reality putting on a performance of "The Pride of the Worm," coming to a church near you. These people become proud of their unworthiness and it manifests into false humility.

Where pride will cause most people to be arrogant and haughty, reverse pride will cause one to react in fear and laziness. This is the case with the servant who was charged with investing a talent of gold. Matt. 25:24 **Then the man who had received one bag of gold came. 'Master,' he said, 'I knew that you are a hard man, harvesting where you have not sown and gathering where you have not scattered seed.** 25 **So I was afraid and went out and hid your gold in the ground. See, here is what belongs to you.'** 26-A **His master replied, 'You wicked, lazy servant!'** God will keep building us up and keep helping us grow toward what He knows we can be. If we keep undermining the word of the Lord and His leading in our lives, we end up in a perpetual saga of crawling like a worm through our Christian life, always a victim and not a victor.

Whether we believe it or not, God

thinks and knows we are His children washed in the blood of His Son and that is our position by grace. We cannot keep saying this is not so by trying a humanistic type of humbleness. We are what the word of God says we are. The sooner we accept that fact and begin to live within the freedom of the word, the sooner we will be like the servant who was given ten talents. We will become the loved children who go on to rule ten cities in humble appreciation of God's grace.

We need to stop this false humility and break forth into the joy of the Lord which is our strength. We need to start singing a new song of belief to our mighty God and savior. Psalm 40:3 **And he hath put a new song in my mouth, even praise unto our God: many shall see it, and fear, and shall trust in the LORD.**

Father, in Jesus name I humble myself by believing what your word says who I am in Christ. Amen.

GET UP

Proverbs 24:16 For a just man falls seven times, and rises up again: but the wicked shall fall into mischief.

The fear of failure is ingrained within us from the first day our loving parents said, "Be careful you don't fall." We might have interpreted these well-meaning words as "Be careful you don't fail." The enemy of our soul is aware of our fear of failure and uses this fear against us regularly. If we are walking circumspect with our Lord then the devil will accuse us of not doing enough for God, trying to get us to trust in our works rather than His grace. Satan points out that we should be just like brother Perfect who prays twelve hours a day and then ministers the other twelve hours without stumbling once.

If we are not walking close with the Lord because of unrepentant sin, then Satan is accusing us of that sin we are struggling with. Hell is bringing pressure upon us to keep doing extra work for God or we are walking in defeat because of a perceived rejection. All this confusion on either side of our relationship is now motivated by fear. No matter what we do, we are being accused by the accuser of the brethren. Rev. 12:10-B **For the accuser of our brethren is cast down, which accused them before our God day and night**.

Thank God for the grace of our Lord Jesus Christ who has delivered us from all performance enhancing rituals to gain the Lord's love and favor. 2 Tim. 1:9 **Who hath saved us, and called us with an holy calling, not according to**

our works, but according to his own purpose and grace, which was given us in Christ Jesus before the world began. How can we have victory without a battle to be victorious over? Why would God give us spiritual armor if we did not need it, or if we were going to leave all the spiritual fighting for our pastor to do? Eph. 6:11 **Put on the whole armor of God, that ye may be able to stand against the wiles of the devil.**

Yes, we will fall. Yes, we will have to decide at that time if we are going to get up. Psalm 37:23 **The steps of a good man are ordered by the LORD: and he delights in his way.** 24 **Though he fall, he shall not be utterly cast down: for the LORD upholds him with his hand.** Get up we will, because we have been given the power to destroy the works of the enemy. Luke 10:19

Behold, I give unto you power to tread on serpents and scorpions, and over all the power of the enemy: and nothing shall by any means hurt you.

We have been filled with the Holy Spirit to discern the deceptions of the devil. Whether we are being tricked into self-righteous works or falling into sin, the Holy Spirit will guide us into all truth. John 16:13-A **Howbeit when he, the Spirit of truth, is come, he will guide you into all truth.** The Spirit of truth working in us is why we are able to get up when we fail and fall. Not if we fall, but when we do we will be able to get up and overcome in the power of His might.

Prov. 24:16-A **For a just man falls seven times, and rises up again.** God is not worried about our falls; He is enthusiastic about our rising up with His grace from the fall to take back that which the enemy of our soul has stolen. Jude 1:24 **Now unto him that is able to keep you from falling and to present you faultless before the presence of his glory with exceeding joy.** The wonder of the cross is that all our sins and failures have been forgiven in full - past, present, and future - and that known fact will keep us getting back up to fight, by faith, from a position of righteousness. We do not have to war from a position of fearing failure because our failures were paid for in full at the finished work of Calvary. John 19:30-A **When Jesus therefore had received the vinegar, he said, 'It is finished.'**

What did I learn the last time I fell? I learnt that if I get up, God's grace and strength is there in full loving abundance to give me the ability to overcome the works of the devil. I learnt that if I get up, God would speak to me. Eze. 2:1 **And he said unto me, Son of man, stand upon thy feet, and I will speak unto thee.** I learnt to get up and get ready for the next battle or test because with Christ I can do all things through Him for His glory and my blessed assurance. We shall overcome. Amen.

EVERYDAY IS A COMEBACK

Proverbs 7:2 Keep my commandments, and live; and my law as the apple of thine eye.

What gives us the ability to get up after a hard knockdown? Why are we so trusting in the love and power of the Holy Spirit within our lives? What is it about the Lord's grace that helps us come back another day to fight the good fight of faith? Lam. 3:22 **Because of the LORD's great love we are not consumed, for his compassions never fail.** 23 **They are new every morning; great is your faithfulness.** That's it saints. The faithfulness and daily renewed love of God towards us compels our hearts to get up and shout, "Praise the Lord for Christ is my victory." 1 Cor. 15:57 **But thanks be to God! He gives us the victory through our Lord Jesus Christ.**

We can all think of someone who once walked with the Lord and has fallen away to make a mess of their lives. We have also heard harsh prognostications of their unlikely return to the service of God because they are too far gone into the world. They are sometimes written off with an unforgiving Pharisaical attitude and with finality. Low tones and whispers are saying, "There is no hope for that son of theirs!" I say, "Not so!" Every day is a comeback day for each and every one of us.

The mercies of God are new every morning. They are for anyone who recognizes their need for a savior regardless of how far down the pit they have fallen. How far can a person fall, you ask? Let's look at the madman of the Gadarene. Here is a man who is possessed with a legion of evil spirits and living a harsh and tormented life. Mark 5:5 **And always, night and day, he was in the mountains, and in the tombs, crying, and cutting himself with stones.** The Gospel of Mark says when he saw Jesus he came running to him and worshipped. Mark 5:6 **But when he saw Jesus afar off, he ran and worshipped him.** I have no idea what had happened to this man's soul to end up possessed by so many evil spirits, but I would think he was in the very bottom of the pit of life; yet Jesus healed and delivered him from his torment. Mark 5:8 **For he said unto him, Come out of the man, thou unclean spirit.** Most likely this man had made the same mess of his life that you see others doing, but the moment he chose to come and ask the Lord for true intervention he was made whole again. The possessed man had to make a choice to be delivered. You cannot force, contrive, manipulate, or cajole a person into healing or rehab per-se. The fallen have to make that choice of their own volition. They have to make the choice to come back and live.

From that day onward, every day would be a comeback day for the formerly possessed man. Every day, this man like us would have to choose righteousness and choose to walk out the word of God in his life. Prov. 7:2 **Keep my commandments, and live; and my law as the apple of thine eye.** We know that there was a true conversion because he wanted to go with the Lord. Mark 5:18 **As Jesus was**

getting into the boat, the man who had been demon-possessed begged to go with him. It is interesting that Jesus trusted what he had done for this man's life because he sends him off on his life mission to declare the mercy and goodness of God to his family. Mark 5:19 **Jesus did not let him, but said, "Go home to your own people and tell them how much the Lord has done for you, and how he has had mercy on you."** In one day this man was a lost cause to society and the next day he has a testimony and is declaring the mercy and goodness of a healing Lord. What a comeback!

Maybe you know someone who has been written off as someone with a heart of granite and it looks impossible for them to repent and come back to the Lord. Don't give up hope because the Lord's mercies and faithfulness are new every morning. God can turn a heart of stone to a heart of flesh. Eze. 36:26 **I will give you a new heart and put a new spirit in you; I will remove from you your heart of stone and give you a heart of flesh.** Maybe you have a family member who had brought hurt, suffering pain, and dishonor to your family. Don't stop praying for them. The Lord of glory has them in His sights; there is a comeback day on the way for them. Isa. 43:1 **But now, this is what the LORD says -- he who created you, Jacob, he who formed you, Israel: Do not fear, for I have redeemed you; I have summoned you by name; you are mine.** We must remember our righteousness is a gift from God and every day is a comeback day for each and every one of us. What an amazing grace Jesus has for us all.

HARD CHANGES

Proverbs 27:1 Do not boast about tomorrow, for you do not know what a day may bring.

One thing you can always count on is change. Sometimes God asks us to do hard things. One of the hardest things He asks us to do is change. Change our minds on something we had our heart set on, but God is saying to let it go. He may ask us to change our attitude toward someone who has hurt us and extend forgiveness toward that person. Mark 11:25 **But when you are praying, first forgive anyone you are holding a grudge against, so that your Father in heaven will forgive your sins, too.** God may ask us to sacrifice ourselves for His sake and the

Kingdom of God. Church history is full of martyrs who gave themselves for us so that we could have the freedom to have a bible or gather together in prayer in a free and open society. John 4:37 **For in this case the saying is true, 'One sows and another reaps.'** 38 **I sent you to reap that for which you have not labored; others have labored and you have entered into their labor.**

Change is happening all the time and all around us. We have no idea what a new day may bring our way. Prov. 27:1-B **For you do not know what a day may bring.** From the earth's orbital seasons to political parties - change happens. From being young to realizing one day we are older. Change takes us along in its current and if we cannot adapt to the changes going on around us we could become despondent and lost.

Business people tell us that change is constant and adaptability is key if the business is to stay viable, relevant, and prosperous. The Lord's church is also changing and hopefully for the better. Remember, we are the church of the Lord and we need to move along with Him when He is moving forward. It was that way in the desert with the children of Israel. When the cloud or pillar of fire moved, the people moved. Ex. 13:21 **By day the LORD went ahead of them in a pillar of cloud to guide them on their way and by night in a pillar of fire to give them light, so that they could travel by day or night.**

With so much change going on, how do we stay stable and secure in the Lord? We are so fortunate to have a God who is constant and continuous in His love toward us. His thoughts and plans for us are victory and blessings. His love never changes toward us. Malachi 6:6-A **For I am the LORD, I change not.** His love is ever-increasing as we grow within His love. You may be going through something right now that seems hard and difficult to change in your life because God is asking you to do it. It can be done no matter what God is asking. No one in history had to go through a change of life events like Noah did. He went from one type of world existence to another entirely different. He went from millions of people on earth to being only one of eight people starting over. When God asked him to build the ark, Noah had to change his schedule and life goals to fulfill what God was asking him to do. Gen. 6:17 **And, behold, I, even I, do bring a flood of waters upon the earth, to destroy all flesh, wherein is**

the breath of life, from under heaven; and every thing that is in the earth shall die. How would it feel to know everything you knew in life was about to be destroyed and you were being asked to be part of the plan?

One thing we can count on is that Jesus is for us and will help us make any of the hard changes we have to do. Heb. 13:8 **Jesus Christ the same yesterday, and today, and forever.** He will give us the strength to accomplish that which we were created for. Phil. 4:13 **For I can do all things through Christ, who gives me strength.** As the Word says, "all things," and that includes change when we have to. Blessing to all who are going through hard changes right now. May God give you grace to do it. Amen.

EVERYDAY FALLIBILITY

Proverbs 21:8 A man is known by his actions. An evil man lives an evil life; a good man lives a godly life.

I had three opportunities to sin yesterday and I passed by two of them. After I repented, I was so proud of my humility. As the Apostle Paul would say, "Oh the wretched man that I am." Why is the heart of man so corrupt? No wonder only the blood of Jesus can cleanse a heart. We have too many layers of deception at work within us; therefore, we should always remember that Christ's sacrifice is the only one that can cleanse absolutely and is acceptable to God the Father. Nothing but the blood of Jesus!

1 Tim. 1:15 **Here is a trustworthy saying that deserves full acceptance: Christ Jesus came into the world to save sinners--of whom I am the worst.** I find it interesting that the Apostle Paul, who wrote so much about being the righteousness of God in Christ Jesus, claimed to be the worst sinner. He continued to understand the power of sin and its nature, also the potential of that nature rising up in our everyday living. Here was a man who had been given revelatory insights into the cleansing power of the blood of Jesus and the resurrection power from the dead by the Holy Spirit, yet would not take his calling in God as a license to sin - so to speak. 2 Cor. 12:2 **I know a man in Christ, fourteen years ago--whether in the body, I do not know, or out of the body, I do not know;**

God knows--such a man, having been caught up to the third heaven. Like Paul, I am so grateful for the cleansing blood of Christ that washes away sin and the condemnation of it. I am also so thankful to God that through the blood of Jesus we have the ability to wrestle the power of sin because we are no longer under the authority of sin. Rom. 8:1 **There is therefore now no condemnation to them which are in Christ Jesus, who walk not after the flesh, but after the Spirit.**

Paul, like us, had to deal with the everyday fallibility that awaits at the doorstep of our hearts. Only the blood of Jesus and the power of the Holy Spirit can keep us in Christ unto eternal life. The older I get the more I see my need for the continual washing of Christ's blood and the righteous standing that comes through it. Not because I am living a life of practicing sin on a perpetual basis, but rather living the fact that only the blood of Jesus can make me whole. Eph. 1:7 **He is so rich in kindness and grace that he purchased our freedom with the blood of his Son and forgave our sins**.

One would think the older we get, the more skilled we would become at not sinning. Not so! The story of the woman who was caught in adultery and was about to be stoned to death shows us that the older we get does not necessarily mean we have a handle on sin and its facets. Jesus says to the crowd, **"He that is without sin among you, let him first cast a stone at her."** At this point something remarkable happens. The scriptural passage says that from the oldest man to the youngest, the crowd dispersed because of the conviction of conscience. John 8:9 **And they which heard it, being convicted by their own conscience, went out one by one, beginning at the eldest, even unto the last: and Jesus was left alone, and the woman standing in the midst**. The oldest and more experienced in life did not have it altogether when it came to a sinless life. The only thing that old age seemed to do for sin was the ability to cover it up with religious antics. It takes the constant covering of God's gift of Jesus' sacrifice to keep us clean in the presence of God. It is not a personal righteousness record that can be boasted about as we come to God in prayer, but it is the gift of God through Jesus that welcomes us humbly before our God. Eph. 2:8 **For by grace are ye saved through faith; and that not of yourselves: it is the gift of God.**

The older I get the happier I am that God has the whole salvation plan under His control. We only have to look around at all the world's confusions to see what man-made religions have caused. Do good, get good. Do bad, get bad. Do nothing, get nothing. Do something, still get nothing. What a mess we create for ourselves when we become our own savior. Jesus, our Savior, accepts us the way we are and turns us into a vessel for His honor because of His works. Yes, my fallibility lurks around me ready to point out my missteps in life, but more importantly I have my Savior who walks with me clearing the landmines that can bring harm to my soul. What a God we serve and what a love He has for us. As long as we live on this earth we will always have the opportunity to fall on our faces because of sin, but thank God that Jesus is right there beside us picking up the broken pieces of our life and turning the same pieces into victory. 1 Cor. 15:57 **But thanks be to God! He gives us the victory through our Lord Jesus Christ.** Thank you so much, Lord Jesus, for all that you do and have done for us. Amen.

THE WORD THAT WORKS

Proverbs 30:5 Every word of God is pure: He is a shield unto them that put their trust in him.

In that moment when we are reading the word of the Lord and the word opens up to our souls and starts to sing a victory song, you know that you know that God has just spoken to your heart, by His Spirit, and you are transformed. There is no doubt that your faith has just been elevated into a holy and joyful realm where you know God will come through for you. Rom. 10:17 **So then faith comes by hearing, and hearing by the word of God.** In effect the Logos or the written word of God has become to your soul the Rhema or spoken word of God and your spirit hears it clearly. Your faith comes alive to say what God has put in your heart to be declared. Mark 11:23 **For verily I say unto you, That whosoever shall say unto this mountain, Be thou removed, and be thou cast into the sea; and shall not doubt in his heart, but shall believe that those things which he saith shall come to pass; he shall have whatsoever he saith.**

In 1982 my wife and I were living in Maroochydore, Queensland. We had been trying to move back to Canada because I had good employment available to me in British Columbia and work was starting to slow down in Maroochydore. My wife had applied for her permanent resident visa with Immigration Canada at the Sydney office in New South Wales. I thought the process might go smoothly because I am Canadian and there was good employment in Canada upon arrival. Well, there was nothing but problems with the process of the application and what came out of the Sydney office was nonsense personified. For nine months there were numerous phone calls and letters written, but this effort brought no help or intelligible advice. During this time I had been reading the word of God, every day, looking for the word that would inspire faith and cause my wife and I to proclaim and make a decree in the name of the Lord that would give us favor in acquiring the resident visa. Job 22:28 **Thou shalt also decree a thing, and it shall be established unto thee: and the light shall shine upon thy ways.**

One morning I was reading the word of God and there it was, the word of deliverance. It came out of my mouth and I knew it was the key that would set faith on fire. I jumped up and said in a loud voice, "In the name of Jesus, let my people go!" That was the word of liberty. John 8:32 **And ye shall know the truth, and the truth shall make you free.** I had been reading Ex. 8:1 **And the LORD spake unto Moses, Go unto Pharaoh, and say unto him, Thus saith the LORD, Let my people go, that they may serve me.** The words "Let my people go," jumped off the page and caused faith to manifest in my soul right in that wonderful moment. I phoned the Canadian Consulate and asked about the visa. With the agent's typical, sterile and insipid voice, she said she would inquire as to the progress of the visa. In that moment I heard the Spirit of God say to my heart, "No matter what she says to you, when she returns to the phone I want you to thank her for doing the very best she could for you." I started rehearsing God's instruction in my heart. I was ready to say, "Thank you for doing your very best for me," when the government' agent came back on the phone. When she picked up the receiver she said, "You know what? You are absolutely correct. This has taken too long. I am getting special permission for this visa today and it will be sent to you." I said, "Thank you for doing your very best for us," as God had instructed. The visa was at our home the next day by overnight courier. Shortly afterward we were living in Kelowna, British Columbia.

The word that works has the ability to give confidence in the love that God has for us. 1 John 4:16-A **And we have known and believed the love that**

God hath to us. When we believe the love that God has for us, our faith becomes Godlike because God is love. We start moving in a Godlike kind of faith because the Spirit of God is directing our faith-filled words. When the spoken word comes from our faith-inspired hearts, there is nothing that can stop it. Isa. 55:11 **So shall my word be that goes forth out of my mouth: it shall not return unto me void, but it shall accomplish that which I please, and it shall prosper the thing whereto I sent it.**

The struggle that people have is overcoming the laziness in finding that God-inspired word that will change the circumstance in their lives. In the case of the visa for my wife, it took us nine months of reading God's word every day while continuing in our Christian walk because the everyday life goes on.

However, we continued faithful until the word of deliverance for that particular need jumped off the page of the holy scriptures. I say no matter how long it takes, it is worth the victory when it happens.

An example of this would be it has been raining every day for two weeks and there is a weariness starting to set in our moods and attitudes. Then one morning we wake up to the most glorious sunny and warm day. We flock outside to do our different activities we have been longing for. You will notice in that moment it does not matter that it had been raining for such a long time, the victory of that sunny day is well worth being alive and full of the joy the day is giving to everyone. The rain is already a distant memory because the victory of the day is huge. Finding the word of the Lord for each one of our situations is like that. It might seem a long time coming, but when it does there will be shouts of praise and gratefulness when we know clearly that the word of God had been fulfilled because of His love for us. John 16:23 **And in that day ye shall ask me nothing. Verily, verily, I say unto you, whatsoever ye shall ask the Father in my name, He will give it you.**

SNAKES AND LADDERS

Proverbs 14:5 A faithful witness will not lie: but a false witness will utter lies.

When your life starts to feel like a game of snakes and ladders it is time to find the word of the Lord for the season you are in, rather than leaving your choices to the roll of the dice. Oh no, you landed on a snake and downward you go. Gen. 3:1-A **Now the serpent was the most cunning of all the wild animals that the LORD God had made.** It might seem like our lives may sometimes run this way, but don't believe it. God said we are the head and not the tail, we are above and not beneath. No saints, we are living under an open heaven with the angels ascending and descending on our behalf. There is a ladder rising into the presence of God through Jesus our Lord. We are seated in heavenly places and we do not have to fear stepping on a snake-oiled slippery slope to destruction when we are under the blessing of the Almighty. Eph. 2:6 **And hath raised us up together, and made us sit together in heavenly places in Christ Jesus:** 7 **That in the ages to come he might shew the exceeding riches of his grace in his kindness toward us through Christ Jesus.**

God is a faithful witness; He does not lie. Num. 23:19 **God is not a man, that he should lie; neither the son of man, that he should repent: hath he said, and shall he not do it? or hath he spoken, and shall he not make it**

good? God's desire is to bless and promote us. He will not lead us on a snake-oiled path where we find ourselves falling away from His love. No! The Lord is constantly trying to get the blessing of the Lord to us because He is for us. God would never have provided salvation for us through Jesus had He been against us. Jer. 29:11 **For I know the plans I have for you, declares the LORD, plans to prosper you and not to harm you, plans to give you hope and a future.** The Lord God does not play a game of snakes and ladders with our heart and emotions. No, sir! He is righteous altogether. Psalm 19:9 **The fear of the LORD is clean, enduring forever: the judgments of the LORD are true and righteous altogether.**

We read the story of Mordecai who had an enemy, Haman. It had become one of Haman's wishes to destroy Mordecai and all the Jews as well. In the book of Esther, chapter 2, Mordecai discovers a plot to assassinate the king and through Queen Esther reveals the plot to the king and saves him. One night the king cannot sleep; he asks for the book of records. Esther 6:1 **On that night could not the king sleep, and he commanded to bring the book of records of the chronicles; and they were read before the king.** The king's servant reads the part where Mordecai had saved the king. The king wants to know if anything had been done for Mordecai. Esther 6:3 **And the king said, What honour and dignity hath been done to Mordecai for this? Then said the king's servants that ministered unto him, There is nothing done for him.** The king decides to honor Mordecai and asks

Haman what should be done for a man that the king wants to honor. Haman, thinking the honor is for himself, tells the king to go all out. Esther 6:8 **Have them bring a royal garment that the king himself has worn and a horse the king himself has ridden, which has a royal diadem on its head.** 9 **Put the garment and the horse under the charge of one of the king's most noble officials. Have them clothe the man the king wants to honor, parade him on the horse through the city square, and proclaim before him, 'This is what is done for the man the king wants to honor.'** The king agrees to Haman's plan, then commands that Mordecai be honored and Haman be the official who leads the horse and procession. Esther 6:10 **Excellent! the king said to Haman. Quick! Take the robes and my horse, and do just**

as you have said for Mordecai the Jew, who sits at the gate of the palace. Leave out nothing you have suggested! Talk about a reversal of fortunes.

What the devil has meant for our harm, God can turn for our good. The enemy of our soul has laid out plans to cause us to fall and falter down a slippery slope of sin and destruction. We can and will overcome all the temptations of the enemy if we stay within and under the covering of our Lord. Psalm 91:1 **Whoever dwells in the shelter of the Most High will rest in the shadow of the Almighty.** You may have fallen down with one of the snakes on your path of life, but be assured there is a ladder right there in front of you named Jesus, the Lord. Grab His hand and climb into a heavenly life God has planned for you.

It is never too late to step up and ask God to help you get up and win. Prov. 24:16-A **For a righteous man falls seven times, and rise up again.** We do not have to play the game of snakes and ladders because our God has determined our salvation through Christ who paid for us in full. Thank you, Lord, for being so good to us.

RIGHTEOUS CHANGE

Proverbs 19:20 Hear counsel, and receive instruction, that thou may be wise in thy latter end.

"But we have always done it that way." This is often said when change is in progress and causing discomfort.

Change is not always easy but often needed to get to the new levels God wants us to grow in. Matt. 9:17 **And no one puts new wine into old wineskins. Otherwise, the skins burst, the wine spills out, and the skins are ruined. But they put new wine into fresh wineskins, and both are preserved.** Under normal circumstances you would feel a bit silly if you were thirty years old and your mother insisted on walking you to the corner store and carrying your money for you. You would say, "Look mom, I am old enough. I'm married with children and responsible with money. I can do this on my own." I say this with tongue-in-cheek. Thank God for all the praying mothers out there. The point is, change is inevitable. If change had not been embraced we would all still be in the old world and the new world would not have been discovered, let alone space exploration and beyond.

The apostle Paul who had been called to bring the Gospel of salvation to the Gentiles had a pit-bull of a fight with the established beliefs of the time. He constantly had to debate the old Levitical-laws and the grace of the new birth offered to all mankind because of the risen Christ from the dead. Phil. 3:2

Watch out for those dogs, those people who do evil, those mutilators who say you must be circumcised to be saved. In essence the New Testament coming into reality was causing the old priesthood to be in a place where they were constantly returning to their vomit or foolishness so to speak. Prov. 26:11 **As a dog returns to his vomit, so a fool returns to his folly.** Their hearts were blind to the moving of the Holy Spirit because they were entrenched in their old and unchangeable ways. Even though God was on the move and bringing in a new dispensation of salvation through Christ, the old guard and their way of doing things had become their folly. They were no longer looking or listened for the leading of Jehovah God whom they professed, but rather dictated to God what His law said and how they would live by it. Inadvertently through traditions, they had pushed God aside and were declaring how to earn righteousness without God's say so. This is a dangerous situation when we start making the bible say what we want it to say so we can rationalize something we know is wrong, but insist in living that way anyways. Jude 1:4 **I say this because some ungodly people have wormed their way into your churches, saying that God's marvelous grace allows us to live immoral lives. The condemnation of such people was recorded long ago, for they have denied our only Master and Lord, Jesus Christ.**

We cannot add impurities to clean water and say it is healthy to drink. Rom. 1:25 **Who changed the truth of God into a lie, and worshipped and served the creature more than the**

Creator, who is blessed forever. Amen. We have to change our minds and hearts to keep our vessels and what is in it clean, because the Lord is righteous and declares what righteousness is. When the Lord brings change to our lives, it is always for the good of our well-being and will still be rooted with the righteous ordinance of His word. The change will not be an allowance for sin just because someone says it is well and legal; therefore, the sin is alright to do now. "After all, we live in this day and age," is what these rebels often say for an excuse to try and legalize their sin. The principles of God's word will always be relevant to its place in history and will always lead people to the Lord's standard and interpretation of His word. The Lord will not lower Himself to a base mindedness just because people want to live in unrighteousness, but rather the Lord will bring us up to His righteous ways. 2 Tim. 2:13 **If we believe not, yet He abides faithful: He cannot deny Himself.**

God Himself does not change. Mal. 3:6-A **For I am the Lord, I change not.** He remains righteous and faithful to His word. He uses His word to change us so that we become like His son Jesus. Don't be afraid of change, whether it is in your church or life. Embrace it because it means we are growing and going forward in the blessings of the Lord and all that those blessings entail. If God has been asking you to change something in your life, then step up to the plate and get it done so that you can say with joy in your heart, "Look what the Lord has done." Be a victor because you said 'yes' to what God is doing in you and not a victim because you put the change on hold. Change is good when God is leading you into it. Blessings.

GRUDGE MATCH

Proverbs 20:22 Do not say, "I'll pay you back for this wrong!" Wait for the LORD, and he will avenge you.

Bob Marley said, "Before you start pointing fingers, make sure your hands are clean."

Do you nurture your grudges like your children? Do you keep them clean and fresh, ready to display as prize possessions at the moment of a woe-is-me opportunity? Why is it so difficult to see the effects grudges have in our own lives and yet so easy to see the effects of grudges in others? This is a common occurrence I run across while in a counseling session with people who just cannot get victory in their Christian lives. It is interesting listening to some of these people express their desire for the judgment of God to take place to someone because of a slight or wrong that has happened to them, yet at the same time claim the mercy and forgiveness of God for their own lives. Mark 11:25 **And when ye stand praying, forgive, if ye have ought against any: that your Father also which is in heaven may forgive you your trespasses.** 26 **But if ye do not forgive, neither will your Father which is in heaven forgive your trespasses.** I know it seems obvious when reading it here on this page, but just not obvious enough when it is happening in one's soul.

Grudges have a way of wearing down the joy of the Lord in a person's heart, the same way sandpaper wears down balsa wood. Unforgiven grudges can show up unexpectedly within a soul out of nowhere. It can be an old photograph peeked at or fragrance on a light breeze that sparks an old angry memory. It can come and sneak up on you like a mugger through a sudden loud sound, or a bad taste when biting into something. Before you know it all hell breaks loose and all because of an old nurtured hurt that has turned into a festering grudge against someone who did you wrong. Gen. 4:23 **Lamech said to his wives, Adah and Zillah, listen to me; wives of Lamech, hear my words. I have killed a man for wounding me, a young man for injuring me.** 24 **If Cain is avenged seven times, then Lamech seventy-seven time.** How far can a person's heart get distorted because of a grudge? In this case the grudge resulted in murder and arrogantly bragging about it.

It does not take much for a grudge to happen, but it takes courage to stop it in its tracks. When someone takes up a grudge and lets it build into something that eventually will control them, it can have long-lasting irreversible effects. We read the story of King Saul putting David in charge of the men of war. 1 Sam. 18:5 **And David went out wherever Saul sent him, and behaved himself wisely: and Saul set him over the men of war, and he was accepted in the sight of all the people, and also in the sight of Saul's servants.** Life is going well, then by chance something happens that causes a grudge to mount up in Saul's heart against David. 1 Sam. 18:6 **When the victorious Israelite army was returning home after David had killed the Philistine, women from all the towns of Israel came out to meet**

King Saul. They sang and danced for joy with tambourines and cymbals. 7
This was their song: "Saul has killed his thousands, and David his ten thousands!" 8 **This made Saul very angry. "What's this?" he said. "They credit David with ten thousands and me with only thousands. Next they'll be making him their king!"** 9 **So from that time on Saul kept a jealous eye on David.** Wow, talk about being insecure. However, it was the words of a song that caused a grudge that would last for years and drive King Saul to make numerous insane decisions concerning the kingdom of Israel. Saul ended up losing everything, including the dedication of his own son Jonathan. Was the grudge worth all the misery brought into a nation and individual families over the rhymes and musical notes of a few dancing girls?

We might laugh at Saul's immaturity, but what grudges are you nurturing that can bring catastrophic effect to your life? There are family members today who will not talk to another member in the family because of something that happened way back in kindergarten. There are people whose grudges have become part of their persona. They make all their decisions based on the hurts they experienced when they were in high school. When is enough, enough? What grudges in your life are worth keeping and disobeying God? Will you be able to bring those well-nurtured grudges into heaven with you? I think not. 1 Cor. 13:4 **Love is patient and kind. Love is not jealous or boastful or proud** 5 **or rude. It does not demand its own way. It is not irritable, and it keeps no record of being wronged.** It is worth noticing that on deathbed confessions, people always want to get rid of the grudge in their lives before they meet their Lord. Why wait so long? Do it now and have an abundant life so that the joy of the Lord is with us now and forevermore. No grudge match is worth winning and definitely not at the cost of our life long peace. Amen!

THE POINT OF NO RETURN

Proverbs 6:23 For the commandment is a lamp; and the law is light; and reproofs of instruction are the way of life.

John 6:67 **Then said Jesus unto the twelve, Will ye also go away?**

The point of no return is normally a technical aviation term in navigation. It refers to the point on a flight when a plane is no longer capable of returning to the airfield from which it took off due to fuel consumption. Major decisions have to be made at that point to ensure the safety of lives and equipment. Literally they are at the point of flying on a wing and a prayer. We all come to a place in life where we make a decision that can be referred to as "the point of no return." As we walk through life and in our faith in the Lord Jesus Christ, there comes a day when we say in our hearts and homes the same thing Joshua said in his day. Joshua 24:15-B **"But as for me and my house, we will serve the LORD."** This statement was Joshua's point of no return.

Jesus had given a very hard word to his disciples and followers. There was a clear doctrine of belief expressed that Jesus was the bread of life and there was no other way to obtain eternal life. John 6:53 **Then Jesus said unto them, Verily, verily, I say unto you, Except ye eat the flesh of the Son of man, and drink his blood, ye have no life in you.** The murmuring was swift and the idea unacceptable to many. John 6:66 **From that time many of his**

disciples went back, and walked no more with Him. At this point Jesus asks the remaining disciples an interesting question. John 6:67 **Then said Jesus unto the twelve, Will ye also go away?** The remaining disciples answer is the answer that comes after realizing they are at the point of no return. John 6:68 **Then Simon Peter answered him, Lord, to whom shall we go? thou hast the words of eternal life.** 69 **And we believe and are sure that thou art that Christ, the Son of the living God.** How true Peter's statement is when he expressed his heart, "You have the words of life, where can we go?" How many times have you come to that place in life where things are very hard and the pressure to compromise seems to be the only option? However, you know in your heart you have already passed the point of no return when you had honestly made Christ the Lord of your life. We may feel trapped and think that compromise is the way out, but if we are mature Christians we will know that Jesus has the words of life for that situation. John 6:63 **The Spirit gives life; the flesh profits nothing. The words I have spoken to you are spirit and they are life.**

Maybe you are facing a difficult situation in your health, finances or relationships and feel you are at the end of your ability to know what to do and the temptation of compromise seems like the only option. Perhaps you feel like giving up on your health. Your excuse to keep using substances you already know are destroying yourself and your family seems a reasonable delusion. The idea of defrauding a company or a person seems justified because the pressures of financial ruin is threatening your ability to bring home an honest wage and theft seems to be a short-term answer. Maybe you are entering a relationship you already know will be abusive and sensually dishonoring all because your fears of being alone and unwanted are a constant reminder. You are not alone. Many are facing the same points of no return in their lives. Matt. 7:13 **You can enter God's Kingdom only through the narrow gate. The highway to hell is broad, and its gate is wide for the many who choose that way.** Instead of compromising, face life with a bulldog tenacity and stick to the leading of the Holy Spirit. We will overcome because the point of no return concerning God's word being our standard will take precedence. There will be a knowing deep in our hearts that

God will come through for us even though we cannot see a way it could happen. Yet in that moment we will know God's faithfulness, but we have to reject compromising our righteousness in Christ. Rom. 8:28 **And we know that all things work together for good to them that love God, to them who are the called according to his purpose.**

There are many hard sayings in God's word that can upset a person and their personal beliefs. We can either stay with the Lord and do what He asks of us, or we can leave Him and go off and trust our own devices. The point of no return is when we act or react to what Christ says. The Lord is either Lord of all or not at all. The choice is ours. As for me and my house, I choose the words Peter so profoundly said. John 6:68 **Then Simon Peter answered him, Lord, to whom shall we go? thou hast the**

words of eternal life. 69 **And we believe and are sure that thou art that Christ, the Son of the living God.** I have made up my mind, I will follow Jesus. There may be times that compromise might seem preferable, but by faith and grace in God's life giving word I will choose life. Deut. 30:19 **I call heaven and earth to witness against you today, that I have set before you life and death, the blessing and the curse. So choose life in order that you may live, you and your descendants.** May we all come to the place where God's word takes precedence in our lives and the point of no return becomes the point of victory. Amen!

PART TWO
FAITH AND BELIEF

Antigua, Guatemala. This door reminded me of the narrow gates we must walk through to exercise our faith.

FAITHFULNESS IN FAITH

Proverbs 31:12 She will do him good and not evil all the days of her life.

Joel Osteen stated, "If we are not faithful in the desert, then how can we be trusted in the promised land?"

A man's word is his bond is still a nice code to live by. Being faithful in all aspects of life is a good goal to fulfill. It might look difficult to live in this world with this type of standard, but with the Lord in your heart it is possible. It may not always be easy, but it is possible. Luke 16:10 **Whoever is faithful with very little will also be faithful with much, and whoever is dishonest with**

very little will also be dishonest with much. We all know someone who has been ripped-off by a scam or a sure deal that could not fail and that person ended up losing their shirt so to speak. What went wrong? Most of the time faith was put into a wrong belief in life, or they misjudged the true character of a person. They ended up putting their entire trust in a human, rather than God. Even a human with the best intentions can get it wrong and that is why we need to keep our heart and mind in Christ. Jer. 17:5 **This is what the LORD says: Cursed is the one who trusts in man, who draws strength from mere flesh and whose heart turns away from the LORD.** This is why we have to build our faith and remain faithful at all costs.

We read about King David making sure his part in a covenant he had made was fulfilled years after Saul and Jonathan's death. It did not matter to David if the other side had kept their part of the deal, he was going to fulfill his part. David asks if there are any descendants left from Saul's family. 2 Sam. 9:1 **And David said, Is there yet any that is left of the house of Saul, that I may shew him kindness for Jonathan's sake?** David finds out that Mephibosheth, a son of Jonathan, still lives but is living in poverty. He is lame from a childhood accident and has a hard time getting around. King David says to bring Mephibosheth to him. David then restores all that was taken from Mephibosheth's family and gives it back to him, plus Mephibosheth would eat at the king's table for the rest of his life. 2 Sam. 9:7 **And David said unto him, Fear not: for I will surely shew thee kindness for Jonathan thy**

father's sake, and will restore thee all the land of Saul thy father; and thou shalt eat bread at my table continually.

Someone might say that King David did not have to keep his part of the bargain because the other side did not keep theirs. When you are faithful in your faith in God, you will keep your part of the covenant because the covenant is not just with the other person but also with the Lord. Christ is inspiring us to do what the Lord has put in our character, no matter what the others do. 2 Tim. 2:13 **If we are faithless, He remains faithful, for He cannot disown Himself.** Faithfulness in faith is not circumstantial but a reality in living. I choose to be faithful because God is faithful to me. I remember a person who had committed adultery and was defending their position for not keeping their part of the marriage covenant because their spouse had committed adultery first. This person was saying, "Why should I keep my part of the covenant when I have been so wronged?" This person thought the sin of adultery they were committing was no big deal because they were only responding tit for tat. All I could think was immaturity comes in all sizes and packages. This person had forgotten that their marriage covenant was not just with their spouse but also with God. Prov. 20:22 **Don't say, "I'll avenge that wrong!" Wait on the LORD and he will deliver you.**

Being faithful in the faith is not just a good idea. While we are on this earth, faithfulness in faith is life itself. On judgment day we will not be standing before God with anyone else. We will be alone with God and the words we want to hear are "Well done my faithful one." No matter how hard some of life's events seem to be, faithfulness at all costs is still a peaceful place to be. God is pleased when we keep getting up and applying faith to any situation. Heb. 11:6 **And without faith it is impossible to please God, because anyone who comes to him must believe that he exists and that he rewards those who earnestly seek him.** When God comes looking for us, will He find us faithful in faith towards Him? I hope so. Luke 18:8-B **But when the Son of Man returns, how many will he find on the earth who have faith?**

LAZY FAITH

Proverbs 20:11 Even a child is known by his doings, whether his work be pure, and whether it be right.

I was talking with a young man who had been raised in a Christian family and had attended church most of his life. He had just now, in his adult life, received Christ as his Savior. We were all blessed and rejoiced with him in his personal salvation with the Lord Jesus. As we talked he wanted to find an easy way to grow his spiritual faith. I said the only way I know of faith growing within our hearts is through the word of God. I explained that faith was exercised through the word of God. As he read God's word and applied it to his life, his faith would grow. Rom. 10:17 **So then faith comes by hearing, and hearing by the word of God.** The young man seemed disappointed because he was looking for an easier way to have a full measure of faith now, this minute. He wanted some kind of "Get faith quick deal." He wanted all the benefits of faith without using his faith. Haggai 1:7 **Thus saith the LORD of hosts; Consider your ways.**

My admonition to this innocent and impatient Christian was that Christianity is not always an easy walk. Our walk with Christ sometimes involves hard decisions like forgiving those who have hurt us, or sacrificing something we want for the sake of someone else. Giving toward a need when we are in need ourselves. Matt. 5:44 **But I say unto you, Love your enemies, bless them that curse you, do good to**

them that hate you, and pray for them which despitefully use you, and persecute you. All these actions take faith and maturity in the faith to accomplish these every day decisions. Yes, there are great and wonderful times of victory as well, but there is no app that we can download or short-cut to a higher game level that will give us immediate faith for what Christ has called us into. This young man, like the rest of us, will have to become personally involved with his personal Lord and Saviour in a personal everyday relationship. He will have to grow in faith as the Lord leads him in his own life's calling. Psalm 143:10 **Teach me to do thy will; for thou art my God: thy spirit is good; lead me into the land of uprightness.**

The good news for this new born-again saint and the rest of us is the moment we even start to send our thoughts in the Lord's direction, He is there. James 4:8-A **Draw nigh to God, and he will draw nigh to you.** The bible says that God will teach us through His word, Jesus. Heb. 1:2 **Hath in these last days spoken unto us by his Son, whom he hath appointed heir of all things, by whom also he made the worlds.** There is great provision for our life's walk with God. We are given guidance, forgiveness, healing, prosperity, correction, love, and everything we will ever need to become the person of God that He saw us to be when He thought of us for the first time. Jer. 1:5 **Before I formed thee in the belly I knew thee; and before thou came forth out of the womb I sanctified thee, and I ordained thee a prophet unto the nations.**

The Lord has put a new song in our

heart and what is in our heart will come out of our mouth. Psalm 40:3-A **He has given me a new song to sing, a hymn of praise to our God.** If we want mature faith coming out of our hearts, then we will have to sow faith, by His word, into our lives so our faith can grow in the grace of our Lord. 1 John 5:4 **For whatsoever is born of God overcomes the world: and this is the victory that overcomes the world, even our faith.** Faith will grow in us by our belief in the word of God and the word of God will produce faith within us as we act on His word. No matter what we do to draw closer to God, we will have to know His word and there is no getting around it. A heartless effort will only produce an insipid faith. The encouraging part of growing in the Lord Jesus is that His grace sustains us as we become more Christ-like and helps us do our best with the faith we have. His priority is our spiritual well-being and His timing in our lives can be trusted. Eccl. 3:11-A **He hath made everything beautiful in his time.**

So, what I practice personally, I advise all impatient Christians to open the word of God every day and be patiently transformed by the word of His love. Acts 13:48 **And when the Gentiles heard this, they were glad, and glorified the word of the Lord: and as many as were ordained to eternal life believed.** 49 **And the word of the Lord was published throughout all the region.**

BELIEVING THE IMPOSSIBLE

Proverbs 3:2 For length of days, and long life, and peace, shall they add to thee.

I was talking with my friend Scott about the lack of faith some of us have toward believing God for an impossible miracle as seen from our point of view. He said, "We tend to pray and believe within our ability to pay, buy, or arrange what we are believing for and therefore the impossible does not happen." We ask God to provide for a situation. If within hours it does not appear, we head out looking for a loan to pay for it. Then when we get the loan we say, "God is good for providing for the situation," forgetting that the word says the borrower is servant to the lender. We do the same with health, family issues and work problems. Num. 11:23 **The LORD answered Moses, "Is the LORD's power limited? You will see whether or not what I have promised will happen to you."** This is a good question God is asking Moses and everyone who claims to have a personal relationship with the Lord. Is the Lord's power limited? In some translations it asks: **Is the Lord's arm too short?** We are all being asked this question. Has God lost His reach and ability on your behalf?

Most of us know that God can do anything He wants. The problem comes when we are asked if God is willing to do it for us personally. Sure, I have no problem believing God would do something for you, but not all that sure if He would do it for me. Therein is the rub. The word of God says without faith it is impossible to please God. Heb. 11:6 **But without faith it is impossible to please him: for he that comes to God must believe that he is, and that he is a rewarder of them that diligently seek him**. I like what Joel Osteen points out in this portion of the verse. For he that comes to God must believe that he is. Must believe that He is what? Yes, we must believe He is God, but more than that, must believe that He is the miracle we are believing for. He is the actual healing we need. He is the provision our families need. He is it! Isa. 43:11 **I am Yahweh, and there is no other Savior but Me.**

We read in the book of Isaiah the story of King Hezekiah who was sick. God said to him through the prophet Isaiah to get his house in order because he would die. Hezekiah prayed and asked God for healing. God tells Isaiah to go back and tell Hezekiah he has granted him another fifteen years of life. God also gave Hezekiah a sign that what God said would happen. Isa. 38:8 **I will make the shadow cast by the sun go back the ten steps it has gone down on the stairway of Ahaz. So the sunlight went back the ten steps it had gone down.** How God did this is full of speculation by biblical scholars much smarter than I am. All I know is that God showed Himself as the God who does the impossible. Joshua asked God to stop the sun from going down so he could win the war. God did as Joshua asked. God did the impossible for him. Are we not getting the impossible things done in our life because we do not ask?

I am at a place in my life where I need

the impossible done for me. I need a new heart that pumps right and regularly. I need a real miracle I cannot buy this afternoon. I need to believe God is what I am believing for. I need the impossible. Well, that is what I am doing. I am believing for a new heart. For the last two and a half years I have done all I can do to take care of my heart and stand in Christ by faith. Eph. 6:13 **Wherefore take unto you the whole armour of God, that ye may be able to withstand in the evil day, and having done all, to stand.** When you have done all to stand, stand firm and let God do the impossible. Someone might say, "Why put so much faith in the impossible? What if it does not happen? I say, "What if it does happen?" What if God gives me the promise in Proverbs 3:2 **For length of days, and long life, and peace, shall they add to**

thee. Thank you Lord, I accept that. Eze. 36:26 **A new heart also will I give you, and a new spirit will I put within you: and I will take away the stony heart out of your flesh, and I will give you an heart of flesh. A new heart of flesh.** I will also take that Lord in Jesus name. If you all could believe the impossible with me for a new heart, I will remember to give God all the glory when it manifests and continually thank Him for all my life. Amen!

THE NAME OF JESUS

Proverbs 22:1 A good name is more desirable than great riches; to be esteemed is better than silver or gold.

I found myself humming and singing an old chorus the other day while working on a project around the yard. ♪ ♬♩ What a lovely name, the name of Jesus. Reaching higher far, than the brightest star. Sweeter than the songs they sing in heaven. Let the world proclaim, what a lovely name.♫♪

God the Father loves the name of Jesus, because it is through Jesus we have been reconciled and restored into relationship with God Almighty. God admonishes us to do more than pay lip service to Jesus, but to actually listen to what Jesus says. Matt. 17:5 **While Peter was still speaking, a bright cloud enveloped them, and a voice from the cloud said, "This is My beloved Son, in whom I am well pleased. Listen to Him!"** Listen to Him is the emphatic instruction given to us because Jesus knows what the Father wants out of our hearts and lives; therefore, pay attention to Jesus and what He says.

The name of Jesus can stir incredible reactions within people, whether positive or negative. What an amazing statement Peter makes addressing the most religiously law keeping scribes, elders, and rulers at the time. Acts 4:10 **Be it known unto you all, and to all the people of Israel, that by the name of Jesus Christ of Nazareth, whom ye crucified, whom God raised from the**

dead, even by him doth this man stand here before you whole. 12 **Neither is there salvation in any other: for there is none other name under heaven given among men, whereby we must be saved.** Peter closes his statement with "Neither is there salvation in any other name." Think about it. The world at that time had gods galore and belief aplenty and God brings to earth one name that can save and do all and beyond any other name imaginable. Jesus is the name above all names, and there is no salvation in any other name. Phil. 2:9 **Therefore God exalted him to the highest place and gave him the name that is above every name,** 10 **that at the name of Jesus every knee should bow, in heaven and on earth and under the earth,** 11 **and every tongue acknowledge that Jesus Christ is**

Lord, to the glory of God the Father.

The power in the name of Jesus was evident while Jesus walked the earth. The Lord had sent out his disciples to minister and deliver people from the bondage and possession of the devil. These disciples came back in the joy of the Lord expressing wonder at the power of Jesus' name. Luke 10:17 **And the seventy returned again with joy, saying, Lord, even the demons are subject unto us through your name.** What a change from the dry and ineffectual religions of the day. In the name of Jesus people were healed, encouraged, and delivered from demonic influences. This caused arguments and debates as to if Jesus had any spiritual authenticity. Then with a resounding declaration Jesus declares, "He is God." John 8:58 **Jesus said unto them, Verily, verily, I say unto you,**

Before Abraham was, I am. Mark 14: 61 **But he held his peace, and answered nothing. Again the high priest asked him, and said unto him, Art thou the Christ, the Son of the Blessed?** 62 **And Jesus said, I am: and you shall see the Son of man sitting on the right hand of power, and coming in the clouds of heaven.**

What an amazing name, the name of Jesus. Within the name of Jesus is the whole plan for man that we would be holy and blameless in Him. Eph. 1:4 **According as he hath chosen us in him before the foundation of the world, that we should be holy and without blame before him in love.** No other name in history can do or accomplish what Jesus did for us on the cross. He became the only sacrifice that God the Father would accept as acceptable for all the sins of mankind. A name above all others. A name I can put my heart, soul, and trust in without fear of being rejected. Oh, Lord Jesus, how wonderful is your name who heals the sick, who calms the storms, who delivers from destruction, and who saves unto eternity. Truly Jesus is the beginning and the end. Rev. 1:8 **I am Alpha and Omega, the beginning and the ending, saith the Lord, which is, and which was, and which is to come, the Almighty.** Thank you, Lord Jesus, for all you have done for me. I am truly grateful.

♪ ♬ ♩ What a lovely name, the name of Jesus. Reaching higher far, than the brightest star. Sweeter than the songs they sing in heaven. Let the world proclaim, what a lovely name.♫♪

BELIEVE GOD

Proverbs 30:6 Don't add to His words, or He will rebuke you, and you will be proved a liar.

James 2:19 **You believe that there is one God; you do well: the demons also believe, and tremble.**

There is the difference between believing in God and believing God. The devil believes in God and trembles, but the devil does not believe God and that is why he continues in his iniquity. When talking with people about God, there is often this statement: "Oh yeah, I believe in God, but I don't believe in the bible or anything like that. After all, Jesus was just a teacher of sorts." This statement is normally followed-up with a weak declaration of non-commitment to anything of faith or value. I do understand when unsaved people of the world talk this way because they do not know the fullness of what God did for them through Christ. But when it is someone who proclaims to be walking in the truth of God's word and living a lifestyle that is contrary to what God says in His word, then we have to look deeper and find the root of the hypocrisy and deception. 2 Tim. 3:5-A **Having a form of godliness, but denying the power.**

When someone is truly struggling with a personal battle of conscience or belief in what God says, a minister might ask, "Since you believe in God, then why don't you believe God Himself and what He says?" There is a difference. When men say they believe in God or that God exists but ignore what God says, they are doing the same thing the devil does; and in some cases without trembling. Until a person starts to believe God, he or she will not leave their iniquitous lifestyle because they believe only in God and that does not take any fortitude or faith. It takes faith to believe what God says and act upon it. To believe in God or that God exists is simply non-committal thinking. Is believing in God and believing God exists a good start to finding God? Yes, absolutely. It is an excellent place to start. But remember, the world is full of people who believe in God but do not do any of the things God says to do to inherit eternal life. We end up in a religious argument with endless semantics. To actually believe God is to do as He says in His word, as in accepting Jesus as Lord - and that is life eternal. Luke 6:46 **And why call ye me, Lord, Lord, and do not the things**

which I say?

Jesus was running into this problem on a regular basis, especially concerning the Sabbath. The scribes and Pharisees would ask Jesus why He and His disciples were breaking the laws of the Sabbath or other traditions. Jesus would then ask the scribes and Pharisees why they ignored God's word to keep their religious laws and traditions. Matt. 15:1 **Then came to Jesus scribes and Pharisees, which were of Jerusalem, saying,** 2 **Why do thy disciples transgress the tradition of the elders? for they wash not their hands when they eat bread.** 3 **But he answered and said unto them, Why do ye also transgress the commandment of God by your tradition?** This line of engagement is a constant discussion throughout the four Gospels in the New Testament. The scribes and Pharisees are constantly touting their belief in God but blinded by their traditions to where they cannot believe God and act upon what God said.

In what is known as The Council Of Jerusalem in Acts 15, we come across an event that sets a precedence for our church history. There was a teaching that had gone out stating that unless a Gentile was circumcised he could not be saved. All the apostles of note got together and hashed out this tradition of Jewish faith and whether this should be expected of the Gentiles. Acts 15:6 **And the apostles and elders came together for to consider of this matter. Peter gets up and says, Look the Holy Spirit has fallen on the Gentiles the same way He did on us. God is judging the hearts of men, not their keeping of traditions and laws that we nor our fathers could**

keep, so why would we put this burden on the Gentiles? Acts 15:10 **Now therefore why tempt ye God, to put a yoke upon the neck of the disciples, which neither our fathers nor we were able to bear?** 11 **But we believe that through the grace of the Lord Jesus Christ we shall be saved, even as they.** A letter is written to be delivered by the elders of Syria and Cilicia where this circumcision doctrine was causing consternation. This is one of the first instructions written in the New Testament, because at this point there are no Gospels or Pauline letters to guide their lives. The word of the Holy Spirit was simply this. In order to follow Jesus and be a Christian per se, start here. Acts 15:28 **For it seemed good to the Holy Ghost, and to us, to lay upon you no greater burden than these necessary things;** 29 **That ye**

abstain from meats offered to idols, and from blood, and from things strangled, and from fornication: from which if ye keep yourselves, ye shall do well. Fare ye well.

The word of the Lord had come through the Holy Spirit and all the Gentiles had to do was believe God and their walk in Christ would start in earnest. The Holy Spirit is saying the same thing to us today. We are blessed to have the whole word of God delivered to us in a collection of books collated in the bible. The word of God admonishes us to believe God and act upon His word for our lives so that we may live a Christ-filled life. If we are believing God and doing what He says, we will not have time to live in sin or empty traditions that bring no peace. Therefore, believe God! Blessings.

A LIVING PROCLAMATION

Proverbs 13:2 A man shall eat good by the fruit of his mouth: but the soul of the transgressors shall eat violence.

I heard Jesse Duplantis say, "Jesus did not explain the gospel, He proclaimed the gospel" Luke 4:18 **The Spirit of the Lord is upon me, because he hath anointed me to preach the gospel to the poor.**

There is boldness that comes upon us when we proclaim the word of God out of a humble spirit. The deep knowing that comes when our proclamation from the word is truly God inspired can be awe inspiring to our soul. The reason this is true is that the Word of God is alive and will not come back void or empty of its assignment. The living word of God will accomplish what God wants it to accomplish. Isa. 55:11 **It is the same with my word. I send it out, and it always produces fruit. It will accomplish all I want it to, and it will prosper everywhere I send it.**

If we could get this principle deep within our heart and mind, we would be proclaiming with boldness the oracles of God without doubt or fear. Since the word of God is in our heart, then as we speak it out of our heart by faith it should have the power and authority to accomplish what God said the word can do. Rom. 10:8 **But what does it say? "The word is near you; it is in your mouth and in your heart," that is, the message concerning faith that we proclaim.** What is holding us back to say what God has said? Throughout the Old Testament we see this principle working all the time. God says to the prophets, "Say to them, thus says the Lord." The prophet would say what God had proclaimed and whatever had been said would come to pass. We have a better covenant and more sure promises in Christ because all the promises of God are yes and amen. 2 Cor. 1:20 **For all the promises of God in him are yea, and in him Amen, unto the glory of God by us.**

Let us not stand back and be spectators of our Christianity, but let us proclaim with joy the word of faith that is in our hearts and be a history maker in Christ. We have a more sure covenant and incredible promises given to us through the power of the Holy Spirit. Jesus says we can have what we say. Mark 11:23 **For assuredly, I say to**

you, whoever says to this mountain, 'Be removed and be cast into the sea,' and does not doubt in his heart, but believes that those things he says will be done, he will have whatever he says. Since Jesus said it, then what He said can be trusted and believed. Let us proclaim the promises of God and see what the Lord will do when we open our mouths and voice His word in His name. Someone might say at this point, "What happens if nothing happens?" I say, "What happens if something does?" God is so good, so let us proclaim His word in Jesus name.

ALL THAT FAITH

Proverbs 13:12 Hope deferred makes the heart sick: but when the desire comes, it is a tree of life.

Our hopes and desires are fulfilled by our faith in God and His word. We know that faith is needed to please God. Heb. 11:6 **But without faith it is impossible to please Him: for he that comes to God must believe that He is, and that He is a rewarder of them that diligently seek Him.** And yet God will allow us, by grace, to approach Him with whatever level of faith we have - even little faith that is close to none. Mark 9:24 **And straightway the father of the child cried out, and said with tears, Lord, I believe; help thou mine unbelief.**

Faith is a gift from God to each one of us, for maturity in the faith to be used for His glory and our growth. Rom. 12:3 **For I say, through the grace given unto me, to every man that is among you, not to think of himself more highly than he ought to think; but to think soberly, according as God hath dealt to every man the measure of faith.** We also know that this faith will increase through believing God's word. Rom. 10:17 **So then faith comes by hearing, and hearing by the word of God.**

There are different types and measures of faith and all faith works in hope of an expected end. Heb. 11:1 **Now faith is the substance of things hoped for, the evidence of things not seen.** The Lord will even help our faith by infusing it with His faith. One of the gifts of the Holy Spirit is the gift of faith from the Holy Spirit. 1 Cor. 12:9-A **To another faith by the same Spirit.**

We are encouraged to use mustard seed faith, with the implication being that the smallest amount of God-inspired faith can move any mountain in our life. Matt. 17:20 **And Jesus said unto them, Because of your unbelief: for verily I say unto you, If ye have faith as a grain of mustard seed, ye shall say unto this mountain, Remove hence to yonder place; and it shall remove; and nothing shall be impossible unto you.** This faith is wonderful because the law of the seed is at work here; therefore, our faith will grow over time if we are patient. I heard a teacher once say, "Even grass turns to milk if you have patience." Likewise, faith turns to substance if we have patience.

As Jesus walked throughout the Holy

land, He looked for people to have faith in Himself. The interesting thing was that He found some great faith with the centurion, the Syrophoenician woman, and the woman at the well. It could be said that this verse describes the faith of these people. Luke 7:9 **When Jesus heard these things, he marvelled at him, and turned him about, and said unto the people that followed him, I say unto you, I have not found so great faith, no, not in Israel.** The other poignant fact is that these people were all gentiles, yet they could see the Messiah clearly and could make a draw by faith on Christ's virtue because their hearts were not clouded with religion as His own people. John 1:11 **He came unto His own, and his own received Him not.** A religious heart will cause our faith to falter, even though every endeavour has been provided for us to come to Him by any faith we have. So let us proceed with His grace, helping us grow in faith, believing from a clean heart. 1 Tim. 3:9 **Holding the mystery of the faith in a pure conscience.**

FAIT ACCOMPLI

Proverbs 16:6 By mercy and truth iniquity is purged: and by the fear of the LORD men depart from evil.

John 19:30 **When Jesus therefore had received the vinegar, he said, It is finished: and he bowed his head, and gave up the ghost.** "It is finished!" is the cry that came from the Lord as He hung nailed to the cross. In that moment to the observer, Christ did not look victorious. He looked like the ravaged victim of the Roman death system that was used to deal with all the trouble-makers of their day. Jesus looked beyond humiliated and degraded, a victim of political circumstance. Even the kingdom of darkness was shaken by their perceived accomplishment;

however, in a short time they realised their tactical error. 1 Cor. 2:7 **But we speak the wisdom of God in a mystery, even the hidden wisdom, which God ordained before the world unto our glory:** 8 **Which none of the princes of this world knew: for had they known it, they would not have crucified the Lord of glory.**

The facts were clear to the onlookers that the man Jesus Christ was dead, but the truth in the kingdom of God was that Jesus Christ, the Lord, had just redeemed man to God. The truth was Rom. 5:8 **But God commended His love toward us, in that, while we were yet sinners, Christ died for us.** There is much to be gleaned from the last words that Jesus said. It shouts to us, reaching our ears today. "It is finished," is the truth we have to come to grips with. It is the truth of the Lord's finished work that will set us free from all the condemnation and bewilderment our hearts struggle with within our faith. As we act on what we believe the will of God is for our lives, we must remember that it is the grace of God that remains the truth we are living in. The fine line of works and grace can cause difficulty in our hearts when we are feeling empty inside. At this point we realise that we have been performing self-righteous acts, thinking we have been obeying our call that was once grace led. We forget that works in the flesh to attain God's favor is finished. Gal. 3:3 **Are ye so foolish? having begun in the Spirit, are ye now made perfect by the flesh.**

The Lord believed His own statement "It is finished" because we read in Heb. 1:3-B **When He had by himself purged our sins, sat down on the right hand of the Majesty on**

high. That's it. The Lord sat down because it had been done and it is done. It is finished! The Lord has done it all and He alone has saved us by His blood and none of our works. Acts 4:12 **Neither is there salvation in any other: for there is none other name under heaven given among men, whereby we must be saved.**

I was going through a tough time and my mind started to wander into the murky and swampy area of works thinking. I started saying things like maybe I feel distant from God because I had those thoughts of jealousy the other day, that's why things are not going well for me. Maybe I did not give enough at church the other day, that's why I lost that deal I was counting on. After all, you reap what you sow. Maybe I had a negative confession in my prayer and I jinxed the flow of provision from heaven. After all, it is a snakes and ladders game we are playing here, isn't it? I do something wrong and I step on a snake and slide downward to a lost place of sin, then I do something good or Godly and climb the ladder of success right into the heavens and then step on a snake to start all over again. This is how a lot of Christianity is lived on a regular basis. We have to realise that God knew this is what we would do, turn His gift of salvation into a carnal works program. Therefore Jesus had to cry out on the cross, "It is finished." Isa. 55:8 **For my thoughts are not your thoughts, neither are your ways my ways, saith the LORD.**

The daily facts that we face are real, but the truth of the word is even more real. The facts are we may be broke, but the word of God says we are blessed and will be provided for. Matt. 6:26

Behold the fowls of the air: for they sow not, neither do they reap, nor gather into barns; yet your heavenly Father feeds them. Are ye not much better than they? The facts are we may be dealing with a sickness in our body and lives, the truth is that we are healed. 1 Pet. 2:24 **Who his own self bare our sins in his own body on the tree, that we, being dead to sins, should live unto righteousness: by whose stripes ye were healed.** The facts are we may be alone in this life and very lonely, but the truth is the Lord is right there besides us. Heb. 13:5-B **For he hath said, I will never leave thee, nor forsake thee.** Matt. 28:20-B **Lo, I am with you always, even unto the end of the world. Amen.** The facts are that we may feel like we have to do something to earn God's love and favor; however, the truth is we are loved and favored - no matter how we feel about it. Rom. 8:1 **There is therefore now no condemnation to them which are in Christ Jesus, who walk not after the flesh, but after the Spirit.** 2 **For the law of the Spirit of life in Christ Jesus hath made me free from the law of sin and death.** Yes, the striving is finished. May the peace of God that passes all understanding fill our hearts with the capacity to believe God's word concerning us all.

BELIEVING BIG

Proverbs 11:18 The wicked works a deceitful work: but to him that sows righteousness shall be a sure reward.

Nelson Mandela said, "It always seems impossible until it's done."

Every new venture or area of life that we have had to move forward in will often seem difficult to accomplish because we look at the task from a position of doing it out of our own strength and know-how. If we remain where we are, then the currents of life will drag us along to obscure and unwanted places. The only way to advance forward in the life God has for us is to get our hearts and thinking in line with God's plan, even if it means we will have to believe big as God does.

Matt. 19:26 **Jesus looked at them and said, "With man this is impossible, but with God all things are possible."** If all things are possible with God, why do we limit His work in our lives with unbelief? Why is Satan so hell-bent on distorting our awesome creativity and well-being in Christ? What is it that God has created in us that makes us so wonderfully unique and well able to soar? These are questions that we will eventually have to answer in order to stretch our faith and start believing for bigger and larger visions in God. The Lord God admonishes us to think and ask for greater abundance in the kingdom of God and enlarge our vision of heart. Isa. 54:2 **Enlarge the place of your tent, stretch your tent curtains wide, do not hold back; lengthen your cords, strengthen your stakes.**

When God asked Isaac to stay in the land that was in famine, what do you think was going through his mind? Gen. 26:1 **And there was a famine in the land, beside the first famine that was in the days of Abraham. And Isaac went unto Abimelech king of the Philistines unto Gerar.** 2 **And the LORD appeared unto him, and said, Go not down into Egypt; dwell in the land which I shall tell thee of:** 3 **Sojourn in this land, and I will be with thee, and will bless thee; for unto thee, and unto thy seed, I will give all these countries, and I will perform the oath which I swore unto Abraham thy father.** God was saying, "Stay in this land and see what I can do with a man in covenant with me and believing for the bigger vision." Isaac obeys the Lord and he sows a crop only to see the miraculous unfold in his life.

Gen. 26:12 **Then Isaac sowed in that land, and received in the same year an hundredfold: and the LORD blessed him.**

What is stopping God from doing the same for any one of us who love and serve Him? Nothing but our own limitations we put on God and His word. God promises His people houses we did not build and vineyards we did not plant. Deut. 6:10 **When the LORD your God brings you into the land he swore to your fathers, to Abraham, Isaac and Jacob, to give you—a land with large, flourishing cities you did not build,** 11 **houses filled with all kinds of good things you did not provide, wells you did not dig, and vineyards and olive groves you did not plant—then when you eat and are satisfied,** 12 **Fear the LORD your God, serve him only and take your**

oaths in his name. When was the last time you asked God for these promises while in prayer?

Many of us have a vision God has put in our hearts, yet we stand around waiting for some kind of burning bush experience to go forward with what God has already told us to do. We become paralyzed with analysis-paralysis, trying to figure out how we are going to do what God has promised us. Meanwhile God is saying, "Hey, I'm over here. Call on me to get this vision going; after all, it is my idea. I want this to work more than you do." We have to stop thinking that we are alone in prayer. Remember, we pray with God and to Him. The Holy Spirit is the one inspiring us to say what God has put in our hearts. The more we speak it out loud, the more real it will become. 1 John 5:14 **And this is the confidence**

that we have in him, that, if we ask anything according to his will, he hears us: 15 **And if we know that he hear us, whatsoever we ask, we know that we have the petitions that we desired of him.**

It is time to believe big and bigger yet. What harm can it do to believe God for the stars? The worst that can happen is you might get the moon and all its' mineral rights. Is there a ministry or passion that has been birthed in your heart? Ask God to set you up to do and fulfill it. Is there a desire to become a mother, business owner, university graduate, pilot, president of a firm or country? Ask big, and ask the only one who can bring the big desire to pass. Get out of the mentality of just hanging in there till the next morsel of blessing comes floating by. No, saints, bring your big dreams to God. He is the dream giver. Then reason it out with Him in earnest prayer because He loves you so much. Isa. 1:18 **Come now, let us reason together, says the LORD: though your sins are like scarlet, they shall be as white as snow; though they are red like crimson, they shall become like wool.** 19 **If you are willing and obedient, you shall eat the good of the land.** Start believing big and let the windows of heaven pour out a blessing that you will have no room to contain it. Amen and amen!

WHOSE REPORT WILL WE BELIEVE?

Proverbs 15:30 The light of the eyes rejoices the heart, and a good report makes the bones healthy.

There are a lot of voices and opinions out in the world that are ready to replace what God has sown in our hearts or said in His word. The question we should be asking ourselves is, "Whose report will we believe?" Isa. 53:1 **Who has believed our report? and to whom is the arm of the LORD revealed?** If God has said it, then we can count on it. There is a war going on in the spiritual realm for our minds and thoughts. God has declared through His word that we are loved and accepted through Jesus Christ. Titus 3:5 **He saved us -- not by works of righteousness that we had done, but according to His mercy -- through the washing of regeneration and renewal by the Holy Spirit.** 6 **God poured a generous amount of the Spirit on us through Jesus Christ our Savior.** God has made it plain that we are His through Christ, yet there is a constant battle of belief going on in the minds of many as to whether they believe the truth of what God said. There is a constant attack on the church and leadership that comes from Satan. The devil promotes doubt and spreads lying rumors to weaken the resolve of God's children. The fact that this happens so fast and regularly shows us that the enemy of our soul cannot handle our faith in the Lord. The moment we believe the truth of God's love, our strength grows and we are able to withstand the lies of the devil. James 4:7 **Submit yourselves, then, to God. Resist the devil, and he will flee from you.**

The word of God continually tells us that God loves us and we are the apple of His eye. Like a loving father, God reaches out to us at all times and makes it possible through Jesus Christ to have an open relationship with Him. Eph. 1:7 **He is so rich in kindness and grace that he purchased our freedom with the blood of his Son and forgave our sins.** The devil comes along and says we must earn God's love and work for His favor. We have to ask ourselves, "Whose report will we believe?"

God tells us that we are saved and blessed. Do we believe it? God says that by the wounds of Christ we are healed. Do we hear and accept it? Isa. 53:5 **But**

he was pierced for our transgressions, he was crushed for our iniquities; the punishment that brought us peace was on him, and by his wounds we are healed. The Lord has said we will prosper in Him as our soul prospers. Is that truth acted upon from our hearts? 3 John 1:2 **Beloved, I pray that you may prosper in all things and be in health, just as your soul prospers.** Whose report will we believe?

The circumstances in our life may look dire, but what does God say about those circumstances? The facts are the everyday events we go through can be challenging. However, the truth is what God says about the overwhelming trials in front of us on our daily walk in Christ. God is truth and there is no lie in Him. What He says to us through His word can be acted upon in full faith and trust. Num. 23:19 **God is not man, that he should lie, or a son of man, that he should change his mind. Has he said, and will he not do it? Or has he spoken, and will he not fulfill it?**

Whose report will we believe? God's report or every other side-show that is out in the world or universe. I believe the Lord loves it when we are believing in Him for the impossible and giving Him the full attention of our heart's faith. I think God smiles on us when we approach Him with the faith of a child and say, "I will believe your report, Lord God!" Heb. 11:6 **Now without faith it is impossible to please God, for the one who draws near to Him must believe that He exists and rewards those who seek Him**

PART THREE TOPICAL

I found this church bell in Antigua. Still used and rings loudly. The Word of God still rings true today.

MISDIAGNOSE

Proverbs 16:25 There is a way that seems right to a person, but its end is the way that leads to death.

I have a friend who has had a very hard two weeks. He was misdiagnosed with a brain tumor. By the end of the first week, neurology discovered it had been a stroke TIA and not a brain tumor after all. As strange as it sounds, there was joy in the family that it had only been a stroke. I thought to myself: "Well, brain tumor in one hand, and stroke in the other. Out of these, choose the best of two evil things." Now the family doesn't know what to believe. Every suggestion for prescriptions and recovery that comes out of the doctors' mouths is suspect. I know the doctors are only human and work within a system that is hectic, overanalyzed, bureaucratically driven and lots of room for human error. The statistics for death caused by misdiagnoses and wrongly prescribed prescriptions is on the rise and becoming frequent. I am not sure what the statistics in Canada are, but the effects of this trend can be overwhelming and concerning to the families it is happening to. As I have stated in the past, I have come to call our medical system "The health-scare system." Perhaps signs of the future. Luke 21:26-A **Men's hearts failing them for fear, and for looking after those things which are coming on the earth.**

Since this type of misdiagnoses is happening in the natural, how many people have misdiagnosed their need for a healthy spiritual life? They come up with overused excuses for not getting involved with God or acknowledging the state of their eternal health. They use the same old lame excuses: the church did me wrong; my family was fanatical and made me go to Sunday-school; our pastor ran off with a member in the church, leaving our family destitute and so on and so on. These excuses come off the tongue like poorly rehearsed lines from a B-movie. Don't get me wrong. There are people who have been severely affected in life with incredible evil atrocities done to them in the name of God, but most often these are not the people in our communities and families spouting-off the usual nonsense about those people down at the church. These acquaintances and family members claim to know all that is knowable about everything Godly. Rom. 1:22 **Claiming**

to be wise, they instead became utter fools. At the end of the day, they misdiagnose their desperate need to be delivered and saved from their sins. God has a word for those who take Him lightly. Rev. 3:17 **Because you say, I am rich, and increased with goods, and have need of nothing; and know not that you are wretched, and miserable, and poor, and blind, and naked.**

A misdiagnoses from the health system may be found out in time and hopefully be rectified by getting on a healing path to recovery. A misdiagnoses of our personal eternal soul can leave us eternally wanting. It will take some humility on our behalf to admit the need for a personal Savior. As the Archbishop of Canterbury says, "Humility is the soil in which pride has difficulty to grow." Don't misdiagnose meek as weak, pride for courage, or vulnerability as gullibility. This type of misdiagnosing has kept people out of the kingdom of God because they thought they knew better than God. Prov. 16:25 **There is a way that seems right to a person, but its end is the way that leads to death.** It takes courage of character to admit the need for help on an eternal scale. It takes an eternal loving God to get us to and through the salvation plan God has for us. Don't let your misdiagnoses or shallow judgment of an infinite God's idea of salvation for your life be guffawed away like some small joke. Our attitude should be from a position of humility and gratefulness when we come to God the Father.

God has given us His grace through Jesus Christ to diagnose our personal need for His salvation plan. Let us humble ourselves unto God and receive His gift with real love and thanksgiving. 1 Pet. 5:6 **Humble yourselves, therefore, under God's mighty hand, that he may lift you up in due time.** I leave you with these words from the book *The Road to Character* by David Brooks. "We sometimes have to crawl into the valley of humility in order to climb the heights of character." God bless you and good spiritual health to us all.

DUNAMIS ΔΥΝΆΜΕΙ

Proverbs 18:21 Death and life are in the power of the tongue, and those who love its use will eat its fruit.

The Greek dunamis is used 120 times in the New Testament. Loosely, the word refers to "strength, power, or ability." It is the root word of our English words dynamite, dynamo and dynamic. Luke 4:14-A **And Jesus returned in the power of the Spirit into Galilee.**

We often feel that we do not have the strength or ability to go forward in what God has called us to do. Yet when we asked Jesus into our heart, we were filled with dunamis power or resurrection power in our innermost being. This is the same power that raised Jesus from the dead. That very Holy Spirit resurrection power lives within each believer in Christ. What is holding us back from moving forward in what God has sown in our hearts? Jesus himself said we would do greater works than he did. John 14:12-A **I tell you the truth, anyone who believes in me will do the same works I have done, and even greater works.** Why would the Lord tell us something that was not so? We have been given the ability in Christ to do what Jesus says we can do in His name. We have been given dunamis power to be ambassadors in the Kingdom of God and to carry on the work that Jesus sent us out to do. 2 Cor. 5:20 **We are therefore Christ's ambassadors, as though God were making his appeal through us. We**

implore you on Christ's behalf: Be reconciled to God.

Resurrection power can heal any disease or mental illness that is known and unknown to man. Jesus was full of this power and He used it to bring about the good news. Luke 8:18 **"The Spirit of the Lord is on me, because he has anointed me to proclaim good news to the poor. He has sent me to proclaim freedom for the prisoners and recovery of sight for the blind, to set the oppressed free,** 19 **to proclaim the year of the Lord's favor."** What is good news to the poor? They will no longer be poor. What is good news to those who are bound with all types of demonic oppression? They will be set free in their bodies and minds. What is good news to the blind? They can see and see well. The dunamis resurrection power will bring us the favor of the

Lord and that is good news. The blood of Jesus cleanses us from all sin, but then we are blessed with resurrection power to grow and be a blessing in life within this lost world. We can be a clear, strong and confident voice for God Almighty proclaiming the good news that Jesus has been raised from the dead and has conquered death for every person who accepts His love and gift of salvation.

When we believe and step forward in the power that God has put within each one of us, we can move mountains so to speak. We read the account of Peter and John through the power of the Holy Spirit healing the lame man who was asking for alms at the gate Beautiful in Acts 3:2 **And a certain man lame from his mother's womb was carried, whom they laid daily at the gate of the temple which is called Beautiful,**

to ask alms of them that entered into the temple. This miracle created a chain of events that would cause Peter and John to be arrested for healing and preaching in the name of Jesus. Peter, through his boldness and dunamis power in heart, leads about five-thousand men to Jesus and causes the Sadducees and priests to lash out in anger to the point of arresting Peter and John overnight. The next day Peter and John are told and warned not to preach in Jesus name as they are released. Acts 4:21 **So when they had further threatened them, they let them go, finding nothing how they might punish them, because of the people: for all men glorified God for that which was done.**

It is interesting that they did not go back to their group and say, "Well that's it you all, we have been shut down. It looks like we will not be able to continue to proclaim the word of the resurrection of the Savior of the world." No! That is not what happened. They got together and were overjoyed at the power of the Holy Spirit and prayed for more boldness to be able to go back out and change the world. Acts 4:29 **And now, Lord, behold their threatenings: and grant unto thy servants, that with all boldness they may speak thy word.** That is what resurrection power can do and will do for every one of us who believe. We do not have to shrink back in fear or anguish. We have been given the power of the Holy Spirit to go out and be the voice and hand extended for our Lord Jesus. May we all pray for boldness to proclaim that Jesus has risen and we have eternal life because of it. Blessings to us all.

DAYLIGHT SAVING

Proverbs 4:18 But the path of the just is as the shining light, that shines more and more unto the perfect day.

The main purpose of Daylight Saving Time (called "Summer Time" in many places in the world) is to make better use of daylight. We change our clocks during the summer months to move an hour of daylight from the morning to the evening. We then take that hour back during the winter months to give us a brighter morning start. We are trying to get as much daylight as possible so we can live a safe and productive life. In fact, we are redeeming the time so we can have more light. If we who live in this natural world can see the need for light and brightness in our everyday existence, then how much more do we need the light of the Holy Spirit to live an eternal life in God? John 11:9 **Jesus answered, Are there not twelve hours of daylight?** If anyone walks in the daytime, he will not stumble because he sees by the light of this world. Jesus was stating the obvious in explaining the difficulty man has in understanding the things of God because of their dark hearts. John 11:10 **But if a man walk in the night, he stumbles, because there is no light in him.** The light of the Lord has to be within a man in order to walk in the light of the Holy Spirit, otherwise man will just stumble through life wondering why everything they do is such a dreary task. Prov. 4:19 **The way of the wicked is like gloomy darkness; they do not know what**

causes them to stumble.

As we get older a regret we often have looking back at our lives is we did not redeem the time well in and at certain times and places. There is no point bemoaning that fact because we did not know what we did not know at the time, and we may not have had the illumination in God we have today concerning certain subjects and events. Today is today. Let us redeem the rest of our time for the love of God and His purposes. Rom. 13:12 **The night is far spent, the day is at hand: let us therefore cast off the works of darkness, and let us put on the armour of light.** Let us walk in the light of this day we have been given and be joyful in gratitude so that we can move forward with the light of God's word in our hearts. Psalm 118:24 **This is the day which the LORD hath made; we**

will rejoice and be glad in it.

The life of Jesus is a perfect example of someone who redeemed the time for the task at hand. We see what can happen when a life is dedicated to the ways of the all mighty God. Someone might say, "We have nowhere near the ability Jesus had when He walked the earth." Yet the word of God says we do have His ability because Jesus lives in us; therefore, all things are possible. John 14:12 **Truly, truly, I tell you, whoever believes in Me will also do the works that I am doing. He will do even greater things than these, because I am going to the Father.** It took Jesus three years and a few followers to change the course of history. Jesus said He would build His church and even hell would not be able to stop it. Talk about redeeming the time and using what was available to Him to change history. All the apostles had to work with was a born-again message that was written on parchments and scripts, but they moved throughout the known world and changed it forever. With the modes of transport available to these dedicated saints, they used what they had and developed rich lives in Christ. How much more effective can we be in the kingdom of God with every possible communication device available to us today if we would just redeem the time in our lives and use them to be history changers.

There is no excuse today for anyone not reading or learning the word of God in order to be a person of blessing in your neighborhood. The Scriptures are available twenty-four-seven if anyone has the capability to stay up that long. Finding time to play games and watch mind numbing television seems easy for a lot of people. Finding time to ask God for His direction and help in a life decision seems to be put off till there is a crises in the person's life. They can rationalize shopping as being easy, but praying is hard. When was the last time you actually talked with God to see what He wanted, rather than showing up in panic mode screaming for help? Thank God we can call for help, but there is more in Christ. When Christ returns for His church, will we be walking in faith and redeeming the time of day? Luke 18:8-B **Nevertheless when the Son of man comes, shall he find faith on the earth?** Redeem the time you have now and develop a relationship with your Lord. Ask Him anything! There is nothing that can shock God as He has been here from the beginning. Walk in the light of His word and God will answer you. Jer. 29:12 **Then you will**

call on me and come and pray to me, and I will listen to you. Thank you Lord for hearing our hearts. In Jesus name!

THANATOPHOBIA

Proverbs 11:19 As righteousness tends to life: so he that pursues evil pursues it to his own death.

Thanatophobia. The fear of death.

This is one phobia we are all going to deal with. I am so grateful to my Lord and Savior Jesus Christ because He has conquered death for us all. Rev. 1:18 **I am the living one. I died, but look—I am alive forever and ever! And I hold the keys of death and the grave.** In North America, where we have been brought up to believe that death is optional, we are awakening to a reality that it is coming one day. As we get older and find ourselves looking in the bible for those long life promises from God, we seem to be cramming for our finals per se. Gen. 6:3 **And the LORD said, My spirit shall not always strive with man, for that he also is flesh: yet his days shall be an hundred and twenty years.** Many are betting on the worst thing said about long life. Psalm 90:10 **The years of our life are seventy, or even by reason of strength eighty; yet their span is but toil and trouble; they are soon gone, and we fly away.**

I believe that all this concentration on the longevity of life is distorting our perceptions of a rich and fulfilled life in Christ. Quality of life comes from having a heart that belongs to God for the purposes of God. The fear of death is magnified when we are not walking in the will of the Lord or just living rebellious lives. When we are at peace with God, then the love of God casts out all fear and that includes the fear of death. 1 John 4:18 **There is no fear in love; but perfect love casts out fear: because fear hath torment. He that fears is not made perfect in love.** 19 **We love him, because he first loved us.** Wow! What a blessing to know that the perfect love of God He has toward us will cast out the fear of death because we are in Him and He is in us.

We do not have to fear our coming death because God will be there right alongside of us, guiding us through the door of death. Psalm 48:14 **For this God is our God for ever and ever: he will be our guide even unto death.** We will step out of this life right into the next one; with God at our side, guiding us through the death experience. In the presence of our Mighty God there is no fear whatsoever. What does this mean? It means we can stare at our grave in the face because the grave has lost its victory over us through the sacrificial work of what Christ has done for us and in us. 1 Cor. 15:55 **O death, where is thy sting? O grave, where is thy victory?**

We read the story of the three young Hebrew men who would not bow down to the golden image that King Nebuchadnezzar set up. The penalty for this act of not worshiping was death by fire in a very hot furnace. There is a blessing in knowing God intimately and it often comes out as calm courage and not as a false bravado. Dan. 11:32-B **But the people that do know their God shall be strong, and do exploits.** The response from the three young men is a spontaneous answer from their hearts. Dan. 3:16 **Shadrach, Meshach, and Abednego replied, O Nebuchadnezzar, we do not need to defend ourselves before you.** 17 **If we**

are thrown into the blazing furnace, the God whom we serve is able to save us. He will rescue us from your power, Your Majesty. 18 **But if not, be it known unto thee, O king, that we will not serve thy gods, nor worship the golden image which thou hast set up.** What did these young men know in their hearts? Maybe it was a word from God that encouraged them to not let fear dominate their souls. Job 14:5 **You have decided the length of our lives. You know how many months we will live, and we are not given a minute longer.**

No one wants to die before their time, myself included. I want a long life of blessed productivity in the Kingdom of God. I want to live a full life that is full of the wonder of my God. The Lord has put before us the choice of life and death and He admonishes us to choose life. Deut. 30:19 **I call heaven and earth to record this day against you, that I have set before you life and death, blessing and cursing: therefore choose life, that both thou and thy seed may live.** Why does He want us to choose life? Because He is life itself and without Him we can do nothing of significance that will have eternal value. 1 Cor. 15:54 **When the perishable has been clothed with the imperishable, and the mortal with immortality, then the saying that is written will come true. Death has been swallowed up in victory.** The fear of death can be conquered by having the life of God manifest in our hearts. Live long and be blessed.

IDENTITY THEFT

Proverbs 12:19 The lip of truth shall be established for ever: but a lying tongue is but for a moment.

Artists work with different paints and mediums to reveal the mysteries of light. They try to obscure darkness with light and contrast, hoping they create a masterpiece or works of art that seduce our hearts and minds to express hidden emotion and unknown feelings. This is one of the things God is trying to do with man on earth; obscure darkness with His light so that we can walk in the light. 1 John 1:7 **But if we walk in the light, as He is in the light, we have fellowship one with another, and the blood of Jesus Christ His Son cleanses us from all sin.** Adam and

Eve were put in the garden to work it and to be artists expressing their hearts and living a good life with a loving God. Gen. 2:15 **And the LORD God took the man, and put him into the garden of Eden to dress it and to keep it.** God was the creator of this garden but man was given free artistic license to display, expand, and enjoy the garden. Then the devil came along and started telling these creative beings who they are and what they want, and we have been looking for identity ever since. Gen. 3:5 **For God doth know that in the day ye eat thereof, then your eyes shall be opened, and ye shall be as gods, knowing good and evil.**

Satan has been stealing people's identity through boldface lying from time and memorial. Remember, the lying devil is also a thief. John 10:10-A

The thief comes not, but for to steal, and to kill, and to destroy. The enemy of our soul is trying to keep us in the dark as to who we are in Christ and what we have in His name. John 10:10-B **I am come that they might have life, and that they might have it more abundantly.** Why does the devil work full-time trying to destroy our identity? We are unique and supreme beings made in the image of the most high, powerful and mighty God that ever was and will be. The devil is frightened of each one of us to a point of absolute eternal despair. The embarrassments, shame, self-hatred and disgust we often feel is the devil's attempt to get us to digest this sickening liqueur, but all this detritus will be pointed at him come judgment day. Rev. 20:10-A **And the devil that deceived them was cast into the lake of fire and brimstone.**

What a day that will be to see the Lord bring true justice and punishment upon the one who actually deserves it. Then God will wash away every tear we have ever shed in shame and the joy of the Lord will be our portion.

Identity in ministry can become a form of idolatry. A few years ago I was wrestling with all the labels that had been put on me throughout my time as a Christian and minister. The Christian community said I was a teacher, pastor, minister, helper, father in the house of God, board member, elder, counselor, leader and on and on it went. I like to think I am just a renaissance man. However, I had become disillusioned with a lot of what was going on in the church. Rather than curse the darkness and lose my identity to some alternative lie the devil was offering me, I did something drastic. No, I did not leave the church. God has planted me in the church to be a blessing to His body. What I did was begin to pray in earnest. I know, what a concept for a Christian to believe in. Phil. 4:6 **Be careful for nothing; but in everything by prayer and supplication with thanksgiving let your requests be made known unto God.**

I was in my office looking at the walls with plaques given to me in gratitude for teaching Bible college and being in Christian service. There were dusty framed parchments that said I was an ordained minister in Australia and Canada. I got up and took every plaque and set of praying hands down and threw them into the rubbish. I took every diploma, pastor's papers, college marks and records and shredded them all. I gathered every essay and paper I had ever written from Bible college to

Bible college teacher and threw them into the recycling bin. I chucked out every sermon on cassette and disc I had ever preached and the notes that went with these sermons were destroyed. I took all my Christian library text books, encyclopedias, dictionaries and commentaries that I had not gleaned anything from in the previous year and gave them to a pastor down the street. I went through my filing cabinets looking for anything remotely ministry-related that I had been a part of and filled the recycling bin to the brim with my so-called identity. Once done I could not find any proof in my office or home that said I had ever been to bible college or had been a pastor, Bible college teacher or minister. It was identity-silent and peaceful.

After my last trip to the rubbish-bin, I came back to my office. Like a gymnast after a routine I stood with my feet together, my posture straight and my hands in the air. I looked to heaven and I said, "Now heavenly Father, who do you say I am?" I smiled at the answer and rested in preparation for the next teaching from heaven and for the next test in life. Phil. 3:14 **I press toward the mark for the prize of the high calling of God in Christ Jesus.** Satan has been lying about our Godly identity. We need to let God give it back to us with a full measure of His love.

PS. I am not advocating that you all run out and destroy all your diplomas. This was something I had to do to get my identification in Christ realigned and find peace in a time of an identity-crisis. It worked for me. Blessings.

ZOMBIES?

Proverbs 12:15 The way of a fool is right in his own eyes, but a wise man listens to advice.

Michel de Montaigne said, "My life has been full of terrible misfortunes most of which never happened."

I was watching a documentary on the apocalyptic fear many people are carrying and living within their lives. The host of the program was interviewing people who call themselves doomsday preppers. The astonishing thing to me was that among these survivalists were people who were preparing for a zombie invasion. There was no doubt in their minds that a zombie type attack was coming. Some said it would happen through a government secret operation or a worldwide medical epidemic, but nonetheless it would happen. What has happened to us as a people? More people are ready today for a zombie apocalypse then they are the second coming of the Lord Jesus. I know Jesus is real and is coming back and I am preparing my heart for that glorious day.

The word of God declared that Jesus would return to earth for those who are His. Acts 1:**11 "Men of Galilee," they said, "Why do you stand here looking into the sky? This same Jesus, who has been taken from you into heaven, will come back in the same way you have seen Him go into heaven."** Jesus said to always be ready and alert for His coming because we do not know the exact time. Matt. 24:44 **So you also must be ready, because the Son of Man will come at an hour**

when you do not expect him. However, people are investing faith, time, and money into zombie preparedness more than they are preparing their souls for the Kingdom of God. There are survival kits, gear, and plans available and promoted on the Internet for defending of home and lands from the inevitable zombie invasion soon to be in a neighbourhood near you. Talk about self-deception and the spirit of fear taking over people's minds. Luke 21:26 **Men's hearts failing them from fear and the expectation of those things which are coming on the earth, for the powers of the heavens will be shaken**.

Since when has the B movie industry and those who continually promote a catastrophic future become an authority on life? Are we becoming a nation of people who believe in nothing and therefore fall for anything? Surely we can do better than a discolored, sunken-eyed zombie to be concerned about. I have no problem with learning how to survive off the grid and re-establishing the outdoor skills a lot of us knew as children growing up. I believe re-educating ourselves to be less dependent on the national grid and government assistance is a good idea. Growing our own healthy food, creating solar and wind power are great skills to have in case of unforeseen emergency. Learning to take care of our spiritual, physical and mental health so that in old age we can still live a life of strength is good common sense. I am not promoting an anti-establishment movement in what I am saying. Live life well and do it in the name of the Lord. Col. 3:23 **Work willingly at whatever you do, as**

though you were working for the Lord rather than for people.

The real concern in life is not being ready when Jesus comes for His church. Will God find us with our hearts full of faith and believing in His redemptive work through the blood of Jesus Christ, or will the Lord find us wrapped up in all the fears of the world? Luke 18:8-B **Nevertheless, when the Son of Man comes, will he find faith on earth?** As for me and my house, we will serve the Lord. It may not be as dramatic as fighting off a colony of flesh-eating zombies, but I'll take the peace that God offers to them who are in Christ. There is enough drama in life without inventing more for ourselves. Matt. 6:34 **Therefore do not worry about tomorrow, for tomorrow will worry about itself. Each day has enough trouble of its own.** Blessing and peace.

ANGER MANAGEMENT

Proverbs 22:24 Make no friendship with an angry man; and with a furious man thou shalt not go.

How is it that we will learn an angry man's ways if we hang out with the angry? It seems that we need some kind of immunization shot against anger in our world today. Things and events easily anger us. Everything from road-rage to all the other rages going on is sapping our kindness and mercy, plus confusing our understanding of righteous anger. We tend to forget that we live in a fallen world, and even though we are not part of it we do live in it. Gen. 4:6 **So the LORD said to**

Cain, "Why are you angry? And why has your countenance fallen? 7 **If thou doth well, shalt thou not be accepted? and if thou doth not well, sin lies at the door. And unto thee shall be his desire, and thou shalt rule over him.** We have forgotten that we need a Savior to give us life and get us victoriously through this present life in order to live with Christ for eternity.

Heb. 12:1 **Wherefore seeing we also are compassed about with so great a cloud of witnesses, let us lay aside every weight, and the sin which doth so easily beset us, and let us run with patience the race that is set before us.** Is there a sin that we keep falling for or into every time it comes along? Is there a sin in our lives which doth so easily beset us? We might say, "Why, Lord, do I fall here every time, and why is this sin so hard for me to overcome?"

Why do some Christians crave drugs, alcohol, gambling, stealing, lying and risky behavior, while others hang on to an unforgiving heart, compulsive disorders, and a dozen other shortcomings? Yet others seem to have no problem with anything listed here? Why am I so weak in one or more of these areas?

In the book of John we read of the woman of Samaria. John 4:7-A **There came a woman of Samaria to draw water.** This woman might have been questioning the same things we have been asking ourselves. Why can't I keep a real relationship with anyone? Why do I have so many insecurities with commitment? Why do I keep falling for the same old lines of promised love? Why do I keep leading all these sappy men on? My friends don't seem to have these problems. I do not know what was on her mind that day, but her encounter with Jesus had a fulfilling result from these words that Christ is offering us today. John 4:14 **But whosoever drinks of the water that I shall give him shall never thirst; but the water that I shall give him shall be in him a well of water springing up into everlasting life.** If we think about it, all the desires that are contrary to what God wants for our lives is a thirst that cannot be quenched with anything offered from the world system. Addictions or obsessions are thirsts within our lives that cause us to go looking for answers and fulfillment in all the wrong places. This cycle of behaviour only deepens the problem and we feel like we are dying of thirst. Meanwhile the very source of life, Jesus, our Lord, is offering us a full cup of life giving fulfillment. Psalm 23:5 **Thou**

prepareth a table before me in the presence of mine enemies: thou anoint my head with oil; my cup runs over.

We read in the Psalms that King David is going through a similar situation. Psalm 73:14 **For all the day long have I been plagued, and chastened every morning.** David is convinced that the suffering of the righteous and the success of sinners has become a reality in his life. However, he comes to a place in his heart where he finds the truth of the matter. Psalm 73:17 **Until I went into the sanctuary of God; then understood I their end.** It is only in the presence of our God that the thirst for all these sins that so easily besets us can be destroyed, washed away, overcome, and forgiven.

Prov. 2:24 **Make no friendship with an angry man; and with a furious**

man thou shalt not go: 25 **Lest thou learn his ways, and get a snare to thy soul.** So, am I just a product of my environment or do I have choices? Where I go to fulfill my thirst is my choice. We do not have to learn an angry man's way and allow it to become a snare to our soul. We do have a way out of the sin which so easily besets us and, thank God, for the love and grace He gives us every day to help us overcome. The Lord admonishes us to drink from His waters of life and our soul will live free. Eccl. 12:13 **Let us hear the conclusion of the whole matter: Fear God, and keep his commandments: for this is the whole duty of man.** In Jesus name, Father, help us always to choose you. Amen.

MALA IN SE

Proverbs 1:16 For their feet run to evil, and make haste to shed blood.

Mala in se is a term that signifies crime that is considered wrong in and of itself. The phrase is Latin and literally means wrong in itself or evil in itself.

It is baffling to me that laws have to be written for some of the most obvious heinous crimes; child slavery, prostitution, abandonment and violence. Imagine, someone actually has to be told that it is evil to beat a baby to death. They do not have the understanding that it is evil in itself to do such a thing. How tragic the human condition that is prevalent in this earth. I was reading some of Philip Yancey's books and he writes about some people in India who deform and cripple children on purpose for the sake of making pitiful beggars of them so that they can bring in some money. Think about it. These people who do this to children have to be instructed that this is an evil practice; therefore, is mala in se. I like to think that I live in a better world than that, but it is not so. A world that has concentration camps, inquisitions and segregation in its history is the real world I live in. The world is influenced by the devil and his wish for mankind is death and destruction, no matter how horrible or tragic the end result is. Jesus said it plainly about the devil's nature. John 10:10 **The thief comes only to steal and kill and destroy; I have come that they may have life, and have it to the full.**

When reading some of the Old

Testament laws I sometimes say out loud, "Really, Lord, you had to write laws and explain to people that they should not have intercourse with animals or their immediate family members?" Is the human condition that pathetic? It must be because God says, "Don't do what the Canaanites do as normal living." A list of instructions is given in Leviticus Chapter 18 that would make commonsense shriek and wonder why this would have to be explained. However, it had to be written so that it would be obeyed. Lev. 18:3 **Do not do what the people of Egypt do. You used to live there. And do not do what the people of Canaan do.** I am bringing you into their land. Do not follow their practices.

These things I have just written about are obviously wrong to most of us. What about the small things that we do on a daily basis? Do we become dulled to the warnings of our conscience that is telling us what we are doing is not acceptable to God? The small lies at work. The stealing of time and goods from work. Shirking from doing a job right. Holding love back from your spouse and children because of a slight you felt you did not deserve. These so called small sins can turn into adultery, larceny, embezzlement and sloth on a major scale to the point that it is odiously mala in se. Gen. 4:7 **If you do what is right, will you not be accepted? But if you do not do what is right, sin is crouching at your door; it desires to have you, but you must rule over it.**

The man who is locked up in prison for embezzling the company did not set out overnight to do so. It started with small thefts that he got away with. The woman or man caught up in an adulterous affair did not set out to bring such hurtful pain to their spouse. Their original heart was not a desire to break their vows made before God and man. No, it started off by wandering eyes and feelings that were not kept under control, resulting in the lust of the eye and the craving of the soul. The result of yielding to small improprieties will eventually bring in a world of hurt. James 1:15 **Then, after desire has conceived, it gives birth to sin; and sin, when it is full-grown, gives birth to death.** What seems controllable and a small indiscretion becomes uncontrolled habitual bondage ruining lives. Just ask anyone who attends Alcoholics Anonymous. It started with one small cocktail, nightcap, or one for the road, until the need for a drink was the most important thing in the universe.

Hurricanes first announce themselves on small scout clouds. Something that has become mala in se in our life most likely announced itself as a bit of sinful pleasure or just a bit of fun and relaxation. We cannot outsmart sin, because the wages of it is still death; no matter how strong and clever you think you are. Jesus is the only one who overcame sin and death. This is why He is the only way through this corrupted world system. John 14:6 **Jesus answered, I am the way and the truth and the life. No one comes to the Father except through me.** Whatever it is that has control of your soul in this life, hand it over to the Lord who knows you and what you need to be healed and delivered. God has us in the palm of His hand. God loves us so much. Amen.

THE HEALTH-SCARE SYSTEM

Proverbs 1:27 When your fear comes as desolation, and your destruction comes as a whirlwind; when distress and anguish comes upon you.

Job 3:25 **What I feared has come upon me; what I dreaded has happened to me.**

I am in my early sixties and I have noticed in general my grandmother's and mother's generation believes absolutely and without question everything the doctor says. My generation, myself included, is very sceptical of what the doctor says and we tend to research everything talked about in the doctor's office. The next generation of forty-something and younger believes nothing the doctor says. I am not sure what this is going to do to medicine as we know it in the near future, but I think a big change will be coming to the whole health-care system as it is presently known. The lack of trust and disbelief in the big pharmaceuticals and their role in influencing the whole medical service plan will have a consequence down the road. This younger (everything is a conspiracy-theory and look out for zombies) generation are finding it hard to trust any type of authority and this is causing fear on an accelerated level. Luke 21:6 **Men's hearts failing them for fear, and for looking after those things which are coming on the earth: for the powers of heaven shall be shaken.**

This past year of my life I have gone through a battle trying to coordinate my doctor, fibrillation-specialist and cardiologist to approach the healing of my heart from a holistic point of view. In the beginning these medical specialists continually tried to sow fear into my heart so that I would accept the multiple prescriptions they were recommending under the standard status-quo of what they normally hand out as health care. I began to call it the heath-scare system because they were trying to instill the fear of every negative possibility that could happen to me during my day and when I slept if I did not take all the pills they were recommending. Gradually all three of my medical professionals started to work with me on a holistic approach when they saw the results from my own healing efforts. Every day and every way

I am getting better. With a lot of prayer and faith in the healing power of God, I have come a long way to a place where I am the healthiest I have been in many years. 3 John 1:2 **Beloved, I wish above all things that thou may prosper and be in health, even as thy soul prospers.**

I think the main reason for the favorable turn around in my health is that I will not buy into the fear that doctors tend to instill in their patients. 2 Tim. 1:7 **For God hath not given us the spirit of fear; but of power, and of love, and of a sound mind.** Every time they tried to push fear on me so that I would acquiesce to modern medicine (which in most cases adds up to taking prescriptions), I would call on the name of the Lord and fight the good fight of faith rather than believe the fearful report. Please don't get me wrong, I do respect the knowledge and years of practicing medicine my doctors have built up in their lives. I also respect their views and the information they have gleaned concerning Atrial Fibrillation: the problem I am overcoming. I am constantly inquiring from their vast amounts of knowledge so that I know what to pray for. However, I will not submit or react to all the dialogue that is fear based and promoted. Phil. 4:6 **Do not be anxious about anything, but in everything by prayer and supplication with thanksgiving let your requests be made known to God.** They can only give me facts about the situation I am in, but God can deliver the truth of His word over the situation and I choose the truth of God's healing word.

Fear is not of God, but it is a main staple within the world. The Lord went to the cross for each and every one of us to deliver us from fear and shame so that we would live in relationship with Him without fear. Luke 1:74 **That He would grant unto us, that we being delivered out of the hand of our enemies might serve Him without fear,** 75 **In holiness and righteousness before Him, all the days of our life.** Whenever we seek the Lord, the first thing He does is deliver us from fear. Psalm 34:4 **I sought the LORD, and he answered me; he delivered me from all my fears.** Every time the Lord presents Himself to anyone in the bible he always says, "Fear not." Some of you may be facing some of your greatest health battles you have ever been in. Know that the Lord is good and He will help you quell your fears and help you overcome the fears of the people you have to deal with so you can defeat the sickness trying to invade your life. Speak words of faith and don't be shy in saying you are strong. Joel 3:10-B **Let the weak say, I am strong.**

Fear is the only weapon the enemy has because he, himself, is full of fear. Jesus is full of love, life and He is fearless. Christ's fearlessness lives within each and every one who has received Him by faith. Do not buy into the fear that is dispensed on a daily basis as if it is a prescription for living. You have the right to reject it because it does not belong to you. Isa. 41:10 **So do not fear, for I am with you; do not be dismayed, for I am your God. I will strengthen you and help you; I will uphold you with my righteous right hand.** As my friend Monica Izaguirre says, " If you are in Christ, then be fearless!" I say, "Amen to that."

TRIAL BY SOCIAL MEDIA

Proverbs 12:20 Deceit is in the hearts of those who plot evil, but those who promote peace have joy.

Sam McGee's view on the negative side of social media might be said this way: "There are cruel things said on the world wide web, by the trolls who spew their souls. Tried and judged with hurtful words, that will make your heart grow old."

How has the mob mentality who post their cruel and hateful thoughts become such a source of read information? Why do people even believe or try to reason with these trolls who post their slanderous and venomous words designed to hurt the wounded, innocent and maybe the guilty? The web has attracted a tabloid type of reporting or as my friend Scott calls it, "lazy journalism." Whatever it is has captured the minds of people who cast judgment without knowledge, factual information, or understanding of events in people's lives. Things that some people say liberally on social media sites, these same people would never have the courage to say to anyone's face. So much of the things said sound like the venting of an adolescent, yet they claim to be of mature age and understanding. Rumors and misquotes are reported as truth and the consequences of this type of free-for-all activity is ignored, regardless of the casualties caused. 2 Tim. 4:3 **A time will come when people will not listen to accurate teachings. Instead, they will follow**

their own desires and surround themselves with teachers who tell them what they want to hear.

It seems the more technologically advanced we get, the less abilities we have to extend compassion or reason. We seem to use the technology to be faster at pronouncing what is in our minds at the split second of hearing a version of an event, regardless of the event being true or false. A person's life can be changed in a day because of what is said about them online. The victim of the millions of digital bytes that are focused on them can be devastating, especially if what is being said is not true. How do you repent or apologize to someone you destroyed online with rumor? Prov. 6:2 **If you have been snared with the words of your mouth, Have been caught with the words of your mouth. 3 Do this now,**

my son, and deliver yourself, when you have come into the hand of your friend; go, humble yourself, and plead with your friend. How do you plead for mercy when you have destroyed your fellow man's life and reputation? It would take some real courage to 'fess up and become a healer of what damage you caused.

The only true and honest man who ever walked the earth got crucified by the self-proclaimed good folk of the same earth. It is interesting that the mob who cried for Jesus to be crucified was provoked by a few envious and political savvy instigators. These rumor-mongers got the crowd riled up with rumors and lies to the point that the everyday person in the crowd was frantically screaming to kill Jesus and release Barabbas. John 18:40 **They shouted back, "No, not him! Give us**

Barabbas!" Now Barabbas had taken part in an uprising. Since the mob mentality had no problem killing the only innocent man ever in the history of the world, I reckon the same mob will have no mercy online where casting judgment can be done with anonymity.

We live in a time when mercy and compassion is needed more than ever. Surely we can abstain from spewing our mental pus on everyday people who messed up or had a tragic event happen to them that was beyond their control. Let us not be so eager to point an accusatory finger of blame because the web makes it so easy to do so. Because of that fact and ease, we should take a moment and think hard about words we are about to express in judgment. Remember the same standard of judgment will be used on each one of us who judges in an unrighteous manner. Matt. 7:1 **Judge not, that ye be not judged. 2 For in the same way you judge others, you will be judged, and with the measure you use, it will be measured to you.** If I was unfortunate to have an unforeseen event happen to me or my family that was beyond my control and then I was publicly blamed for it, I know that I would desire mercy and understanding just like every one of you. When it comes to social media, I will remember the Lord's words as to what is expected of me in life. I hope you take them to heart as well. Micah 6:8 **He has shown you, O mortal, what is good. And what does the LORD require of you? To act justly and to love mercy and to walk humbly with your God.**

PART FOUR
SELF-CONTROL

In Antigua this door brought this scripture to mind: Revelation 3:20 Behold, I stand at the door, and knock: if any man hear my voice, and open the door, I will come in to him, and will sup with him, and he with me.

TAKE MY OWN ADVICE

Proverbs 2:9 Then shalt thou understand righteousness, and judgment, and equity; yea, every good path.

1 Corinthians 9:27 **But I discipline my body and keep it under control, lest after preaching to others I myself should be disqualified.** It sure is easy to give out advice, but another thing to live the advice being offered. The word of God is constantly admonishing us to make sure that we put into action what we are preaching. If we do not do as we preach, then we become self-deceived. James 1:22 **Do not merely listen to the word, and so deceive yourselves. Do**

what it says. It is so easy to say what should be done and then not proceed to do it ourselves. We have to be aware that we do not simply pontificate to achieve a status as a great orator and end up with no substance of heart. Jesus was having to bring this sin in the open on a constant basis. The Scribes and Pharisees were excellent at public showings, but bankrupt when it came to the substance of their souls. Mark 12:40 **Yet they shamelessly cheat widows out of their property and then pretend to be pious by making long prayers in public. Because of this, they will be more severely punished.**

It is always so disappointing to the general public when a sport phenom or member of the privileged authorities ends up morally crashing because they were caught doing the very opposite of what they claimed their lives stood for.

Many a person who had been preaching an honest lifestyle ended up caught up in a scandal or embezzlement scheme that hurt a lot of the citizens. Rom. 2:22-A **You who say that people should not commit adultery, do you commit adultery?** It is such a let-down to our idea of what is right that discouragement steps in to create a state of abandoned helplessness. Psalm 12:1 **Help, LORD, for no one is faithful anymore; those who are loyal have vanished from the human race.** We have to become men and women of our word and stick to it even when it might cost us time, money, or something of value. Matt. 5:37 **Just say a simple, 'Yes, I will,' or 'No, I won't.' Anything beyond this is from the evil one.**

As I write this I am preaching to myself because I need to take my own advice and do what the Lord and His word has taught me to do. It is so easy to say, "Love the sinner but hate the sin." The sentence just rolls off my tongue with little human effort, but am I able to put it into practice? The word of God clearly says to pray for our enemies and for those who sin against us. Great theory and easy to say, but to actually do it? Matt. 5:44 **But I say unto you, Love your enemies, bless them that curse you, do good to them that hate you, and pray for them which despitefully use you, and persecute you.** Ouch! I'm going to need your help here, Lord. Someone said, "Opinions are like belly buttons. Everyone has one." I venture to say that advice is similar: everybody has some. May we all become people of substance and truth and live our own advice.

Peter had to make a decision whether

he was going to follow his own advice. His public declaration that he would never forsake Jesus came back to bite his ego very hard. He had to deal with his own hypocrisy. After living the bitterness of that experience, he recommits his heart to the Lordship of Christ and becomes an apostle of renowned. From that point on Peter begins to take his own advice to heart and live what he is being taught by the other apostles and the Holy Spirit. We know this because in Galatians chapter 2 Paul confronts Peter for his hypocrisy concerning eating with the Gentiles and the negative influence his hypocrisy caused. As time goes by, Peter again changes his heart and attitude toward the fact that God is for all mankind and not just the Jews.

Doing what the word of God says to do is how we become skilled at following our God-inspired advice. When we follow our conscience that is dedicated to the Lord, we will be able to take our own advice with a confidence that comes from God. May the advice I give come from a practiced, proven, and lived lifestyle that gives honor to God and my fellow man. In Jesus name!

A STRONGMAN'S WEAKNESS

Proverbs 25:16 Hast thou found honey? Eat so much as is sufficient for thee, lest thou be filled and vomit it.

I heard someone say, "Too much of a good thing will cause us to eventually lose interest and dislike whatever that good thing was." I say too much of anything that is not God-led will become commonplace and will lose its shine, no matter what the good thing is. The Lord must be in our daily choices or we will even become ungrateful for what we abundantly have today that was lacking years ago. Deut. 6:12 **Be careful not to forget the LORD, who**

rescued you from slavery in the land of Egypt.

When I was 16 years old I worked in a men's clothing store and we would save the shoe boxes that customers did not want. Once we had accumulated twenty-four boxes, we would then trade the shoe boxes with the bakery next door for a dozen honey dip donuts. The bakery would use the shoe boxes for packing box lunches for the pipeline construction-crews working the area. For me in 1968 donuts were a wonderful and rare treat, but since then the shine has come off of them because donuts are not a rare specialty anymore. You can throw a stone and hit a Tim Horton's or a dozen other type of donut drive-through windows at the whim of fat cells screaming for a crispy cream. Deut. 8:11-A **But that is the time to be careful! Beware that in your**

plenty you do not forget the LORD your God.

What happened to the rare treat? Donuts had become commonplace and lost their special rarity to an over-abundant surplus from our consumptive demand. This common surplus has happened to almost everything consumable in the world. In a short amount of time, what was once unique and special is poured out in truck-loads at the nearest box depots. I am not complaining. I am just observing a trend that can easily lead to a spirit of entitlement, then eventually leading to an ugly case of ungratefulness.

Even a strong Christian can get caught up with all the offerings from the altars of the worldwide everything on sale stores. Mark 3:27 **No man can enter into a strong man's house, and spoil his goods, except he will first**

bind the strong man; and then he will spoil his house. Thank God that in our weakness He is strong and gives us the armour of God to protect ourselves from the tricks of the enemy who tries to destroy us. Eph. 6:10 **Finally, my brethren, be strong in the Lord, and in the power of his might.** 11 **Put on the whole armour of God, that ye may be able to stand against the wiles of the devil.**

How do Christians keep themselves walking as a strongman? I don't believe a vow of poverty or joining a monastery is the answer. No, the answer is within us. Jude 1:20 **But ye, beloved, building up yourselves on your most holy faith, praying in the Holy Ghost.** How can we make everyday living special again? 1 Thess. 5:18 **In everything give thanks: for this is the will of God in Christ Jesus**

concerning you. Some might say that I have a Pollyanna view of looking at the overwhelming worldliness invading our Christian lives. Not so. I say the written word of God in its simplicity is still the only thing that can get us through the valley of the shadow of death while keeping us strong. The cleansing blood of Jesus that washes us from all sins in this world is still the only healing salve that gives us the right to call on the name of the Lord to work His miracle needed in our lives. Isa. 47:4 **As for our redeemer, the LORD of hosts is his name, the Holy One of Israel.** True, I am a strongman of God who falls in weakness, but my God is strong all the time and nothing is impossible for Him. Jesus is Lord!

SELF DELUSIONS

Proverbs 19:21 There are many devices in a man's heart; nevertheless the counsel of the LORD, that shall stand.

Definition of delusion: A delusion is a false belief that is based on an incorrect interpretation of reality. A person with delusional disorder will firmly hold on to a false belief despite clear evidence to the contrary.

As strange as it sounds, the above definition seems to be describing the world system and all the beliefs that go along within it. The word of God says that the heavens declare the glory of God, yet God is not believed or even acknowledged. Psalm 19:1 **The heavens are declaring the glory of**

God, and their expanse shows the work of his hands. When unbelieving man wants to be a denier concerning the existence of the only wise God, then he himself chooses to be delusional in his response to the obvious facts of God's creation staring him in the face. God never debates with the unbeliever, whether God is or is not. God simply says to have a taste of Him and they will know where the blessing of life is. Psalm 34:8 **Taste and see that the LORD is good; blessed is the one who takes refuge in him.** These people choose self-denial and self-delusion in order to live the way they want; without code in life or responsibility of life toward anyone or anything. They think they can protect themselves from hurts and grief by simply rejecting the responsibility of life that sometimes brings challenging and emotional events. They are basically saying, "I do not acknowledge God; therefore, I am free from His expectations of me." Rom. 1:21 **Because that, when they knew God, they glorified him not as God, neither were thankful; but became vain in their imaginations, and their foolish heart was darkened**.

In the early 1980's I was ministering in the prisons of New South Wales, Australia. I met a lot of inmates who had convinced themselves it was the fault of others they were incarcerated. They sometimes rationalized that they had little to do with the fact that they had robbed the bank, stolen the cars, or had committed other crimes. They were always sorry for getting caught, and if they had another chance they would not get caught the next time. This self-delusional conversation went on most of the time. When I did meet people who took responsibility for their actions, the outcome was very different. When these people were released from prison, most of them had productive lives.

We do not have to be a criminal to be self-delusional. The fanatical religious can be as delusional as seen with Jim Jones to Osama bin Laden. When there is a corporate scandal of immense thievery in the billions of dollars, self-delusion and greed are most often the reasons for the outright thefts as seen in corporate America over the years. Government ministers who fall from grace per se as in their misconduct in office because of adultery, embezzlement, or hubris often are delusional because they think they are above the laws of their own country. They have talked themselves into thinking they can break the law of God and man without consequence. Spiritual leaders who fall under similar circumstances think they have acquired some kind of spiritual get out of jail free card for their shameful actions. Gal. 6:7 **Do not be deceived: God cannot be mocked. A man reaps what he sows.** There is grace and forgiveness for all the above sins and thank God for that. However, there are consequences in life for all the choices that are made by each and every one of us. Deut. 30:19 **I call on heaven and earth as witnesses today that I have offered you life or death, blessings or curses. Choose life so that you and your descendants will live.** Therefore, let us be forthright in our choices.

God asks us to have our minds renewed with the word of God, because God's word is what will help us overcome deceptive visions of grander inspired by self-delusions. Rom. 12:2 **Do not be conformed to this world, but be transformed by the renewing of your mind. Then you will be able to discern what is the good, pleasing, and perfect will of God.** God's word strongly imprinted in our minds will help us know what God wants for our lives because the word of God will eventually make its way to our heart and we will know what to do in life. We do not have to be mesmerized by every whimsical and delusional idea that floats by. We can make intelligent decisions toward life and all the intricacies that it offers. We will be able to discern between good and evil and not crash our lives while trying to figure out difficult decisions. Heb. 5:14 **But strong meat belongs to them that are of full age, even those who by reason of use have their senses exercised to**

discern both good and evil. In essence, we will be able to grow up in the Lord and in our thinking. 1 Cor. 13:11 **When I was a child, I spake as a child, I understood as a child, I thought as a child: but when I became a man, I put away childish things.** Look for the wisdom of the Lord and grow in His grace. God is our hope and we need not be ashamed, because the word of God is the power of our salvation and life. Rom. 1:16 **For I am not ashamed of the gospel, because it is the power of God that brings salvation to everyone who believes: first to the Jew, then to the Gentile.** Believing in God's word is not delusional, it is righteous and good living. Amen.

INFAMY

Proverbs 25:10 Lest the one who hears it put you to shame and your infamy will never go away.

Infamy: the state of being well-known for some bad quality or deed. The evil fame we are known for.

The proverb says, "Your infamy will never go away." There is a truth in this because many people are known by what they did wrong, even though they spent the rest of their lives trying to do right and overcome the mess that made them of evil fame in the first place. Great ministries, CEO's and politicians that have fallen terribly have been remembered for the shame and evil fame, rather than the efforts they made to turn their lives around and go straight so to speak. Thank God for the grace of God and that God judges the heart of man, not on his past failures, but on the merit of the blood of Christ. The Grace of God is amazing because the evil fame we became known for can be replaced with an identity of who we are in the Lord now, even though mankind may not be on board with God's proclamation of who you are. Rom. 8:1 **So now there is no condemnation for those who belong to Christ Jesus.**

In 2 Samuel chapter eleven, we can read the story of King David and Bathsheba who committed adultery. The adultery results in Bathsheba getting pregnant. King David tries to fix the problem by having Bathsheba's husband come home on military leave in the hopes of a conjugal visit, but Uriah does not go see his wife; therefore, King David arranged the murder of Uriah to cover up the adultery and pregnancy of Bathsheba. Sounds like an episode of bad reality TV. This infamy never left David and Bathsheba; however, God saw David as a man after God's heart. Acts 13:22 **But God removed Saul and replaced him with David, a man about whom God said, 'I have found David son of Jesse, a man after my own heart. He will do everything I want him to do.** David was quick to repent and keep going with God regardless of what had been done. Psalm 25:11 **For the sake of your name, LORD, forgive my iniquity, though it is great.** Yes, the fruit of what had been sown would cause problems in the kingdom of Israel and Judah. The evil fame of the sins David committed would always be a fact in David's life, but with God there is forgiveness and the opportunity to live in the favor of God regardless of the infamy David was known for.

I am not making light of adultery or murder, or any other heinous sin committed on earth. I am saying you might have committed something difficult for mankind to forgive and as the proverb says, "Your infamy will never go away." This may be the way it is for the rest of your life, and be sure the devil will remind you of this fame at every opportunity that presents itself. However, God has the last word and commentary as to what He will say about you throughout eternity once you repent. That is the power and forgiveness found through the blood of Jesus. God will still use the calling on your life for His purpose, even though you might have ruined your good name through the action you took to become labeled with the infamy. Rom. 11:29 **For**

the gifts and the calling of God are irrevocable.

I have known and know some people dealing with the label of infamy attached to them; it is like an appendage that sticks out, no matter where they go. As some of you know, my respect for some of these fallen one's has waned. However, the love of God must be offered and granted to them the same way the love of God has been given to us; unconditionally. The warning we get in the word of God is also clear. We must watch our hearts in judging, lest we fall in the same places and end up with an evil fame of our own. Gal. 6:1 **Brothers and sisters, if someone is caught in a sin, you who live by the Spirit should restore that person gently. But watch yourselves, or you also may be tempted.** Let us live our lives with the goal of walking circumspectly before God and our brothers and sisters in Christ. Let us do our best not to become another statistic of infamy. God bless you.

NO ONE FALLS ALONE

Proverbs 7:22 He goes after her straightway, as an ox goes to the slaughter, or as a fool to the correction of the stocks.

There have been some people who have walked with God for years and have taken a hard moral fall in this past year. These are people we know and we pray for a Godly recovery and restoration. God does say in His word that He would bring judgment to the church first. God's heart is to clean us up to be a real testimony to the world. 1 Pet. 4:17 **For it is time for judgment to begin with God's household; and if it begins with us, what will the**

outcome be for those who do not obey the gospel of God? One of the things I have noticed in these unfortunate moral breakdowns is no one falls alone. Regardless of the depth or severity of the sin that was practiced or taken up, there are always casualties other than the person who has fallen. I have seen firsthand the effects of the sinful shrapnel that brings devastation and wounds to many in the body of Christ.

Many people think they are hurting no one but themselves if they alone are practicing sin in private, or acting out just under the radar of public noticeability. This is such a lie because we are all connected in the body of Christ. No one lives and dies unto themselves. 1 Cor. 12:21 **And the eye cannot say unto the hand, I have no need of you: nor again the head to**

the feet, I have no need of you. We need each other in Christ. This is not some new revelation that we are suddenly noticing. King David was dealing with the pain of losing a friend because of a sin that betrayed a relationship. Psalm 55:12 **For it was not an enemy that reproached me; then I could have borne it, neither was it he that hated me that did magnify himself against me; then I would have hid myself from him:** 13 **But it was you, a man my equal, my guide, and my close friend.** Whether or not the fallen are close friends or mere acquaintances in the body of Christ, it still hurts the souls of everyone who walked with these people and it hurts in the deepest parts of our being.

I thank God there is healing for this type of hurt. I am also so grateful that He can and will restore those who have fallen if they ask for forgiveness. We have to realize that the fallen could have been ourselves. If I had fallen into the deepest despair of sin, I would be thrashing for forgiveness like a drowning man would be thrashing to survive. Our hearts hurt for these brothers and sisters who fell short, but we also intercede for their recovery to faith and stability in Christ. There is grace for all of us. 1 John 1:9 **If we confess our sins, he is faithful and just to forgive us our sins, and to cleanse us from all unrighteousness.**

The lesson I have taken from these painful life circumstances and the devastating effects on others is to keep my heart available to God's scrutiny, asking Him to point out potential pitfalls. Psalm 139:23 **Search me, O God, and know my heart! Try me and know my thoughts!** In this world and times, I don't know any other way to keep clean in heart but to stay circumspect before God and my brothers and sisters in the church body. Allow God to correct our lives daily and submit to the correction. May we all be able to say as Paul did. 2 Tim. 4:7 **I have fought the good fight, I have finished the race, I have kept the faith.** Lord God, keep us all and help us see clearly the steps before us and may we run the race with your strength. In Jesus name.

LIFE'S PROSTITUTES AND IDOLS

Proverbs 29:3 Whoso loves wisdom rejoices his father: but he that keeps company with harlots spends his substance.

God gave a straight and forward commandment to mankind. Ex. 20:3 **Thou shalt have no other gods before me.** This eight word commandment is clear and without doubt as to its meaning. No other gods means just that, no other gods! Yet many of us live our lives prostituting ourselves with other gods. We don't think of them as gods or see them positioned on street corners as in some

Eastern cultures, but nonetheless they are all around us. The dream home, dream car, dream vacation, and the dream spouse and so on are the gods of our time. You might say, "I don't bow down and worship these things in my life." I say, "Just think back to the last argument you had with God about sacrificing that something God had pointed out was in danger of becoming an idol in your heart." Was it easy to say, "Yes, Lord, I give it up freely." If it was not easy to hand over that god or idol, then there is another god in your life. Matt. 22:37 **Jesus declared, "Love the Lord your God with all your heart and with all your soul and with all your mind."**

You might be in a checkout line at a grocery store and the magazine rack conveniently at eye level will display a variety of modern day goddesses and advice on how you can become one. Aphrodite the Greek goddess of love and all her tentacles with her worldly interpretations of love are available for the price of your soul. Hand over your well-earned money to this goddess who will promise you true love and attraction for ever. Paul the Apostle says that real love does not boast, brag or gloat and yet the foundational success of Aphrodite and her promises of erotic love are built on the very things Paul says is not real love. 1 Cor. 13:4 **Love is patient, love is kind. It does not envy, it does not boast, it is not proud or rude.** 5 **It does not demand its own way. It is not irritable, and it keeps no record of being wronged.** In our time Aphrodite has wreaked havoc with the hearts and souls of young people whose body images do not line up to her so-called perfections and values for acceptance. However, the Lord loves us the way we are and actually helps us become His unique person. Rom. 5:8 **But God demonstrates his own love for us in this: While we were still sinners, Christ died for us.**

Tyche, the Greek goddess of fortune and prosperity, has overruled our good senses to the point of seduction and falling for so-called free money. This easy wealth is available to us on a scale never seen in history. Individuals with half a million and million dollar plus debt is no longer uncommon. The goddess of prosperity has given us lavished privileges, promises, and assurances that over-extending our ability to pay off debt is no big deal. She says, "Don't worry, just trust me and I will bail you out in time." Not so! The word says clearly, the borrower is the servant and slave of the lender. Prov. 22:7 **The rich rules over the poor, and the borrower is servant to the lender.** Enslaving ourselves to Tyche will make us ineffective in the kingdom of God. Our energies and commitments will be elsewhere because our thoughts will be consumed with the pressures of debt. This idol of prosperity shines bright in the beginning, but soon we find out she is made of fool's gold. Let God be your master of true prosperity and you will come out as pure gold. Mal. 3:3 **He will sit like a refiner of silver, burning away the dross. He will purify the Levites, refining them like gold and silver, so that they may once again offer acceptable sacrifices to the LORD.**

Ares, the Greek god of war, has offered us trophies and assurances of success if only we would become workaholics and indulge in cutthroat business practices trying to become number one. Ares asks us to sell ourselves to him so we can be listed as the billionaire of the year on the cover of some fortune magazine. You can be the top dog as long as you crush everyone you meet along the way, because all is fair in love and war. If you don't take care of yourself, then who will? You had better get all you can now, no matter what the consequences. Ares has no mercy for his followers and for what the Lord is trying to build in our hearts. Gal. 5:22 **But the fruit of the Spirit is love, joy, peace, patience, kindness, goodness, faithfulness,** 23 **gentleness, self-control. Against such things there is no law.** The law of Ares is slash and burn and take no prisoners, but the law of God is set the prisoner free. John 8:36 **So if the Son shall set**

you free, you will be free indeed.

These prostitutes and idols have made their way into our world and lives by cunning and stealth. We cannot defeat them on our own by simply trying to take them down. We must replace them entirely with the one Lord and Savior Jesus. When Jesus is reigning on the throne of our heart, then we will have the power to tear down strongholds that try to become the idols of our heart. 2 Cor. 10:5 **Casting down imaginations, and every high thing that exalts itself against the knowledge of God, and bringing into captivity every thought to the obedience of Christ.** There is only room for one God in our heart. May it be the Lord of lords and the King of kings. God bless you.

MODUS OPERANDI

Proverbs 21:15 It is joy to the righteous to do justice; But it is a destruction to the workers of iniquity.

Disraeli said, "Life's too short to be little." We often get caught up in the everyday events of life in this fast moving world. Sometimes we forget we are building our lives upon an eternal foundation. 1 Cor. 3:11 **For no one can lay any other foundation than what has been laid down. That foundation is Jesus Christ.** We put our energies and strenuous thoughts into a comfortable retirement and forget our God-given goals of eternal reward. I know we have to live on this earth, but we still have to choose where we want to spend eternity and what we want to give of ourselves toward the kingdom of God. Let's face it, eternity is a long time to exist in regret or damnation for that matter. There is a day when our life's work, or for some people their life's ministries, will be judged at the Judgment seat of Christ. What we have sown in our Christian life may not be of Godly quality or valuable. 1 Cor. 3:13 **But on the judgment day, fire will reveal what kind of work each builder has done. The fire will show if a person's work has any value.** What were our motives for all the work done in the Lord? Was the work done to establish the kingdom of God or our own kingdom built of hay and stubble? 1 Cor. 3:12 **Now if any man build upon this foundation gold, silver, precious stones, wood, hay, stubble;** 13-A **Every man's work shall be**

made manifest.

Our motives are just as important as the work itself. The Apostle Paul warns us to be aware of people whose motives are suspect. Rom. 16:17 **Now I beseech you, brethren, mark them which cause divisions and offences contrary to the doctrine which ye have learned; and avoid them.** 18 **For they that are such serve not our Lord Jesus Christ, but their own belly; and by good words and fair speeches deceive the hearts of the simple.** In another Scripture John the Apostle warns of similar corrupted motives that are not the will of God, nor are they His motives toward the people of this earth. 3 John 1:9 **I have written something to the church, but Diotrephes, who likes to put himself first, does not acknowledge our authority.** 10 **So if I come, I will bring up what he is**

doing, talking wicked nonsense against us. And not content with that, he refuses to welcome the brothers, and also stops those who want to and puts them out of the church. The motivational gifts God gave us are for building up the body of Christ and not tearing it down by our own misuse or misguided motives. Our motives are just as important as our heart's desires in Christ.

We do have to ask ourselves if our modus operandi toward the works of God are led by the Holy Spirit. Is our manner, technique or approach to God's leading just a belligerent attitude of "Take it or leave it God. You get what you get and you should be happy with that." Is working His eternal plan just an irksome task we grudgingly slog through? If our relationship in the Lord has reached this sad point, then it is possible our motives toward eternity has already changed to a place of desperation and loss. As I said, "Eternity is a long time to suffer loss."

Saints, we need to get our hearts back to thinking and reaching for the eternal prize and reward that awaits us. Phil. 3:14 **I press on toward the goal to win the prize for which God has called me heavenward in Christ Jesus.** The joy of the Lord is our strength and with that strength we can enter His gates with thanksgiving in our hearts. When our motives are clean, our ministry and calling will be joyful and motivated. Righteous motives will get the work of God done and our hearts and lives will be full of eternal joy. The Lord tried to admonish Cain to change his motives and attitude so there would be peace in his life. Gen. 4:7 **If you do well, will not your countenance be lifted up?**

And if you do not do well, sin is crouching at the door; and its desire is for you, but you must master it. The result of Cain not submitting to God's word was a loss of relationship with God and man. Life is too short to waste it on missing the mark God set for our well-being. What is God's motive for mankind? That should be our motive as well. May God give us a new vision of His will. Amen!

A FOOL'S ERRAND

Proverbs 28:26 He that trusts in his own heart is a fool: but whoso walks wisely, he shall be delivered.

As the ship was tied up to dock side in Tangier, it became clear that we were not only miles from home but also centuries from our time. Dark and weathered dock workers dressed in caftans and single-loop sandals were tying the ship to the dock. Some of these old crusty men had fez hats, while others wore colourful customary beanie caps. Livestock of all sorts were being lowered by archaic winches, pulleys, and tackle. Old carts drawn by beasts of burden were hauling away large baled bundles of goat skins. Gurgling sounds came from the protesting camels as they were led away carrying loads of exotic goods. The heat fermented an aroma that ponged as it attacked the nostrils to the point of nausea. Gangplanks were drawn for foot passengers to carefully make their way down to the old dock. As we walked off the passenger ramp, our passports were stamped and visas issued by the sweaty men in worn out customs uniforms that dated back to the second world war. It was a scene from "The Curse Of The Mummy's Tomb" and there we were, traveling Morocco, looking for spiritual enlightenment. In 1971 my friend and I were eighteen years old and traveling throughout Europe and Morocco. Many of my contemporaries were doing the same and traveling as far as the Middle East and India. So many travelers at the time were looking for spiritual enlightenment, but most of them came home disillusioned and suffering with dysentery. 2 Tim. 3:7 **Ever learning, and never able to come to the knowledge of the truth.**

Many people, then and now, are looking for God on their own terms. They want a God that they can control and, therefore, write the rules to their own lives. Isa. 29:13 **Wherefore the Lord said, For as much as this people draw near me with their mouth, and with their lips do honour me, but have removed their heart far from me, and their fear toward me is taught by the precept of men.** When things go wrong, like a shooting in a school, these same people are normally the first to complain about the Godlessness exhibited in their homeland today. Yet they are the ones who wrote the new gospel of trusting in our own hearts (this is my truth, and that is your truth) and the result manifesting as a group of fools wondering why the God of eternity does not do something. Hag. 1:9 **Ye looked for much, and, lo, it came to little; and when ye brought it home, I did blow upon it. Why? saith the LORD of hosts. Because of mine house that is waste, and ye run every man unto his own house.**

We, as a solipsistic society, will rationalize and spin anything to our own heart's belief and desire, even when we know it is not true. We have been led to believe that trusting in our own hearts (our own manifesto) is the way to accomplishing our dreams, but many have found their personal nightmares instead. Lam. 5:15 **The joy of our heart is ceased; our dance is turned into mourning.** From investing into a scam that first appeared the best deal of the century, to marrying the wrong person who turned out to be a wife-beater, they question what went wrong? We were trusting in the selfishness of our hearts and not the Spirit of God's guiding of our hearts by His word. Jer. 17:9 **The heart is deceitful above all things, and desperately wicked: who can know it.**

A heart that is not owned or occupied by the Lord can be deceived and led astray because there is no confidence of heart or understanding of God's wisdom. We need, by faith, to believe that God's will and purpose in our hearts is a good thing. Eze. 11:19-A **And I will give them one heart, and I will put a new spirit within you.** If we are having a hard time believing that God's thoughts toward us are pure and a blessing, then it will be difficult gaining the confidence we need in God to live our lives in this precarious world.

John 14:1 **Let not your heart be troubled: ye believe in God, believe also in me.** Jesus said He was the only way to God. I would rather trust Jesus than my own heart's patch-work of syncretism trying to make everything fit to my liking. This fallacy of belief will eventually lead to disillusionment and dare I say it: "Spiritual dysentery." There are already too many winds of doctrine that lead people astray without adding to them. I am content to be in the Lord's hands, being led and loved along the way. Sng. 2:4 **He brought me to the banqueting house, and his banner over me was love.**

MY EGO IS TROUBLE

Proverbs 29:23 A man's pride shall bring him low: but honour shall uphold the humble in spirit.

Whenever I climb I am followed by a dog called "Ego." Friedrich Nietzsche.

In 1980 I heard Julie Buchenauer say, "Don't let your milestones become millstones." She preached to the effect that we can get caught up in our own good works and miss the next blessing, because we have become enamoured with our milestones in life and they now start turning into millstones grinding us to limited growth. Her statement marked me well because I have lived by its advice. Whenever I got proud of something I thought was great in my life, I would enjoy the blessing of it but after a while that old saying would needle its way into my mind and I would say out loud, "Don't let your milestones become millstones, time to move on to the next thing God has for you." Phil. 3:13 **Brethren, I count not myself to have apprehended: but this one thing I do, forgetting those things which are behind, and reaching forth unto those things which are before,** 14 **I press toward the mark for the prize of the high calling of God in Christ Jesus.**

I heard Wayne Dyer say that "ego" was an acronym for Edging God Out. This is true in my life. I get into problems when I start twisting God's instruction into my own ideas. I start edging God out and doing things my way when the results are not as fast as I think they should be and my ego won't let me see my folly. 1 Sam. 25:25-B **Nabal is his name, and folly is with him.** Sometimes we just have to admit that we were wrong in a decision made. Yes, we were sincere, but we were sincerely wrong. We start asking God to bless something that was never His intention. Abraham wanted God to make Ismael the son of promise, but God wanted His covenant done right. Gen. 17:18 **And Abraham said unto God, O that Ishmael might live before thee!** 19 **And God said, Sarah thy wife shall bear thee a son indeed; and thou shalt call his name Isaac: and I will establish my covenant with him for an everlasting covenant, and with his seed after him.** Ishmael (the milestone) had become a millstone around Abraham's neck. Abraham was stuck on an idea that would not work and the progress of his life was grinding to a halt until he agreed to send Ishmael and Hagar away. The millstone that Abraham was carrying was hindering the blessing of the Lord from going forward in Abraham and Sarah's life.

Someone said, "When ambition ends, happiness begins." I would say, "When personal obsession ends, happiness in God begins." Eccl. 10:1 **Dead flies cause the ointment of the apothecary to send forth a stinking savour: so doth a little folly him that is in reputation for wisdom and honour.** We can become a stench to the Holy Spirit when we are riding our egos toward the promise land and believing our own press rather than being dependent upon the leading of the Lord. We start looking at our milestones and thinking, look what I have done for God, isn't He blessed to have me doing all those extras for Him? Before we know it a millstone has pressured us into making unrighteous decisions and we start believing the end justifies the means. We do not have to look far back in recent history to see this effect. A few TV evangelists came to a disastrous end because of poor choices and dependency on their media name brands, rather than the power of the Holy Spirit. Was restoration and healing available for them? Absolutely, and thank God some of them accepted God's forgiveness, but what hurts and loss could have been avoided had ego and pride been dealt with. Thank God for His grace toward us as He keeps drawing us back onto His track of a narrow and righteous walk. Psalm 30:11 **Thou hast turned for me my mourning into dancing: thou hast put off my sackcloth, and girded me**

with gladness.

It comes down to this. Let us enjoy our victories and milestones in life because God helped us get them. However, do not let them become what we worship and turn them into idols. Eccl. 12:13 **Let us hear the conclusion of the whole matter: Fear God, and keep his commandments: for this is the whole duty of man.** 14 **For God shall bring every work into judgment, with every secret thing, whether it be good, or whether it be evil.** Father, in Jesus name, help us all be stronger in Christ and in the power of His might rather than our egos.

LESS THAN HONEST

Proverbs 20:10 False weights and unequal measures—the LORD detests double standards of every kind.

I heard the statement "less than honest" being used to describe a person's character. I thought we are either honest or dishonest, but not less than honest. Here we go again minimizing the effects of sin and the fallen nature of man. We use a double standard of spiritual measurement when it comes to wanting to simplify sin in our lives. He is not a thief, he just has sticky fingers. She is not a prostitute, she is just a lady of the night. We are not liars, we simply embellish our position or we misspeak. He is not dishonest, he is just less than honest. I think God would call this fig-leaf-religion. Gen. 3:7-B **And they sewed fig leaves together, and made themselves aprons.** We use aprons to cover our sins and to cover our momentary faux pas. See, I'm doing it, turning a sin into a small misstep; a simple faux pas.

Where does this less than honest approach to the human condition come from? Why are we so devious? In the book of Jeremiah, a profound statement is made about the heart of man. Jer. 17:9 **The heart is deceitful above all things, and desperately sick; who can understand it?** That is the problem. Our soul's default setting is duplicity at best and subterfuge at worst. We just cannot fix this heart condition on our own. That is why we need a savior. Thank God for Jesus and the work He did for us on the cross. Our hearts have been made clean through the blood and sacrifice of Jesus our Lord. Nah. 1:7 **The LORD is good, a stronghold in the day of trouble; and he knows them that trust in him.** Outside of God's help to create a new heart within us, there is no help. Man's heart is deceptive and needs an absolute reconstruction made by God.

Jesus understood this about our human nature. Christ is at work continually on man's heart. Through His teaching of parables and lessons, the Lord reveals our motives in life. Jesus' nature and example for living was pure and God-centered. He did not need man's approval for His mission on earth. Jesus made sure He did not fall into the trap that popularity brings, but kept his purpose God-minded. John

2:23 **Now while he was in Jerusalem at the Passover Festival, many people saw the signs he was performing and believed in his name.** 24 **But Jesus didn't trust them, because he knew human nature.** 25 **He did not need any testimony about mankind, for he knew what was in each person.** Dare I say it, Jesus knew that mankind was less than honest.

Growing into and reaching for a mature heart that is God-centered is the will of God for each one of us. No half-measures can be used to find the heart and will of our heavenly Father. Jer. 29:13 **And ye shall seek me, and find me, when ye shall search for me with all your heart.** I suppose seeking God with a half-hearted approach would be less than spiritually honest on our part since God tells us to do it with all our hearts. Perhaps living an insipid milky-toast Christianity is also less than forthright when it comes to being ready to give an account of the real hope that we live in because of what Christ did for us. 1 Pet. 3:15 **Instead, exalt the Messiah" as Lord in your lives. Always be prepared to give a defense to everyone who asks you to explain the hope you have.** We have been saved from a Christless eternity. Wow, there is a reason to seek God with a full, exuberant, and hopeful heart. Maybe giving it all we have for the Lord will keep us all truly honest and become people of character in Christ. May we all be an honest blessing to man and God.

PART FIVE
FORGIVENESS

Forgiveness reflects what's going on inside of our heart. 16th. century window frame in Antigua, Guatemala.

I AM SO SORRY!

Proverbs 16:24 Gracious words are like a honeycomb, sweetness to the soul and health to the body.

I'm sorry. I apologize. I was wrong. Please forgive me. These words are some of the hardest to say because the fallen human condition is, by default, fearful of being wrong and fearful of appearing to be weak by saying it. In this era of quick and pithy comebacks or one-upping one another, saying "I'm sorry or I was wrong" does not sound cool or get the shallow gratification that comes from up-staging another human being. Most often those who take pleasure in the downfall of others are full of fear themselves and their antics are masks to cover their cowardice hearts. 2 Tim. 1:7 **For God has not given us a spirit of cowardice, but of power, and of love, and of self-control.** Nonetheless, we are often wrong and need to come to the reality that being wrong is not a shameful thing. As a matter of fact, it is most often the way we learn a new thing in life.

One of the freedoms of being in Christ is that Jesus gives us the ability to overcome the fear of being wrong through His redemptive work that is available for each one of us who has accepted Him as Lord. Saying "I'm sorry" to man or God does not sit well with most of the human population because of the fear of appearing weak. This is why pride is so destructive to the human soul. Pride insists on having its own way and will make man do some of the most terrible things to one another.

We see this pride at work on the battlefield of Israel. David's oldest brother, Eliab, sees David talking with the men about the situation concerning Goliath. Eliab starts to belittle David with hurtful words, then he tries to one-up him through shame and sarcasm. Everything Eliab is accusing David of is the very thing Eliab is acting out of his own heart and soul. 1 Sam. 17:28 **When Eliab, David's oldest brother, heard him speaking with the men, he burned with anger at him and asked, "Why have you come down here? And with whom did you leave those few sheep in the wilderness? I know how conceited you are and how wicked your heart is; you came down only to watch the battle."** Basically paraphrased, "You're just a small sheep herder of no significance. You're not a super soldier like I am." There definitely is no room for the words "I'm sorry" in Eliab's vocabulary. Why? Because it takes humility and courage to apologize and repent for the hurts we have caused. The Archbishop of Canterbury said, "We sometimes have to crawl into the valley of humility in order to climb the heights of character. Humility is the soil in which pride has difficulty to grow."

A few years ago my wife asked me to pick up a couple of things she needed at the grocery store. It was early in the morning and quiet except for the musac that numbs the senses if you actually listen to it. There were three cashiers open and two of them were at one end of the frontage of the store and one was at the far end. As I walked by the one who was alone, I was struck with such aching and crying of heart that I almost collapsed. The cashier was the exact duplicate in facial image, hair color, size and age of a girl I had shamefully humiliated in high school. In that moment the truth and understanding of what I had done over forty-five years ago to her wounded soul was palpable and real as if it were yesterday. I said to God, "Oh Lord, I am so sorry for the way I treated her. I want to ask her for forgiveness if I could." Then I felt the Lord say, "Go and ask the cashier if she will stand in proxy for the girl you humiliated." Num. 32:23 **But if ye will not do so, behold, ye have sinned against the LORD: and be sure your sin will find you out.** There were still no customers around her so I went up to her and said, "This might seem strange, but you are the exact duplicate of a girl I went to high-school with." I then went on to confess my sin and explain to the young cashier why I needed forgiveness and I asked her if she would stand in proxy for her and forgive me. She actually said, "I stand in proxy for her and I forgive you for what you did." The weight of the world came off my shoulders in that moment and I thanked the Lord for His goodness.

I believe what took place in the spirit that morning was twofold. I was set free and I truly believe whatever effect my terrible treatment had on the young lady was also healed in her from the hurt I had caused. John 8:36 **Therefore, if the Son sets you free, you really will be free.** This feeling of being set free for both of us was a deep knowing in my soul. God is so good. Don't ever be afraid to say, "I am sorry." It truly is liberating. Prov. 16:24 **Gracious words are like a honeycomb, sweetness to the soul and health to the body.** God bless you all.

FORGIVE ME, PLEASE

Proverbs 8:1 Doth not wisdom cry? and understanding put forth her voice?

"I forgive you. Completely." This is the answer that should come from our lips, but most often these words do not make it past our mind because we are not ready to forgive completely. We want God's grace and forgiveness in our own lives, but we want the judgment of God on those who have harmed us. I was talking with a married couple who were talking about something that had happened over twenty-five years ago. In the middle of the sentence the woman turned to her husband and said, "Don't you remember that time when you called me a #@!!#$@?" He looked at me with that look that says, "When is this ever going to be forgiven? I have apologized for this every time she brings it up." I wanted to leave the room because you could cut the air as they say. I do not believe she knew how to just let it go or hand it over to God, allowing Him to dissolve the memory in her hurt. It was causing a strain in their relationship. 1 Cor. 13:5 **Love does not dishonor others, it is not self-seeking, it is not easily angered, it keeps no record of wrongs.**

Forgiving, completely, is just that; completely forgiving the wrong, just as Christ forgave us completely and entirely. Col. 3:13 F**orbearing one another, and forgiving one another, if any man have a quarrel against any: even as Christ forgave you, so**

also do ye. We might have to say it out loud a few times to get use to the words, "I forgive you. Completely!." Again, "I forgive you. Completely!"

It is wisdom to forgive completely. How do I know that? God is pure wisdom and He forgave everyone completely. Now through His Son Jesus Christ we can accept forgiveness and be at peace with God and ourselves. If God forgave us completely, then this is the right thing to do. God asks us to be forgiving as He is. Rom. 5:8 **But God demonstrates his own love for us in this: While we were still sinners, Christ died for us.** Someone will say, "This is easy for you to say, forgive completely. Just try and forgive what I have been through." I'm sorry, but that argument does not work. There will always be someone on earth who has gone through unthinkable hurts and violations beyond our imagination. These people have experienced something worse than the next person. If that is the measurement, then nothing will ever be forgiven as it will only create an argument as to who hurts more than the next person and nothing will get fixed and no opportunity for repentance will ever be available. God says to step up to the plate and be the first to forgive, then the real blessing of Christianity will start. Eph. 4:32 **And be ye kind one to another, tenderhearted, forgiving one another, even as God for Christ's sake hath forgiven you.** When did the blessing of the new birth start? After forgiveness came through the cross. First there was the desire of forgiveness in God's heart, then He sent Jesus to be the atoning work that gave us His forgiveness.

The wisdom of God compels us to

forgive, because the nature of His Son Jesus now lives within us. Just take a close look inside your heart when you allow anger, rage and declarations of revenge with that someone who has done a terrible thing to you. Do you have God's peace? Do you have your joy? Do you even have your blessed assurance? No, because you are no longer that old character you once were before Christ started changing your heart. You cannot go back to that way of thinking without losing something of quality in your soul. 2 Cor. 5:17 **Therefore if any man be in Christ, he is a new creature: old things are passed away; behold, all things are become new.** Will this be hard for some? Yes it will be, but oh the power of God that comes from forgiving the one who kept you miserable. There will be no more reasons for the blame-game that the enemy of your soul keeps reminding you of. The moment you forgive, you will also destroy the works of the devil. No wonder he helps you remember your hurt. James 4:7 **Submit yourselves therefore to God. Resist the devil, and he will flee from you.**

Think of that person who needs your forgiveness and say out loud, **"I forgive you. Completely."** Keep saying it until you believe it, then enjoy the Lord's peace in your soul. Blessings.

GETTING EVEN

Proverbs 24:29 Do not say, "I'll do to them as they have done to me; I'll pay them back for what they did."

When it comes to getting even with someone who has hurt or betrayed our personal pride, feelings, or even injured our body, the downward spiral of evenness can only bring more hurt than the original offense. The problem with getting even is the process always brings a person down to a lower level of existence of being because the original offense or slight was already a low blow. You end up at the bottom with the bottom feeders, so to speak, and coming back up to where the Lord is trying to mature your soul can be a hard and arduous time. This is why God says vengeance is His affair and not ours to take into our own hands. God knows the right judgment for the offender and the right cure for those affected. God's purpose is to get both sides into a righteous plan of love and honor. God understands the discipline needed for the offender and the right curing ointment for the the one who got hurt. Satan wants us angry at the world so that we become a reactionary and violent people, continually living is a state of craving vengeance. John 10:10-A **The thief comes not, but for to steal, and to kill, and to destroy.** At this point madness creeps into our once peaceful lives and we become unhappy victims of offense.

How can grace work if retaliation is the constant automatic response? History shows us the effects of keeping grudges alive and festering. The oozing open sore of hurt pride will only put the next generation on a course of prejudice and bitterness. Eze. 18:2 **Why do you cite this proverb when you talk about Israel's land: 'The fathers eat sour grapes but it's their children's teeth that have become numb.'** The children suffer because forgiveness is not a part of their everyday life. Families who are always looking to get even forfeits the freedom of forgiveness. By this time vengefulness reaches a generational feud, then getting even is no longer the point and the atrocities become greater. We can see this in our recent history with the fallout from World War II and the festering hurts that came up again in the Kosovo conflict of the 1990s. It will never stop until someone says, "I forgive you and I do it with the grace of God." Luke 6:28 **Bless them that curse you, and pray**

for them which despitefully use you.

We read in the book of Genesis the story of Lamech whose pride had been hurt to the point of dictating the amount of pay back that would be satisfactory to his self-importance. Gen. 4:23 **Lamech said to his wives, "Adah and Zillah, Listen to my voice, You wives of Lamech, Give heed to my speech, For I have killed a man for wounding me; And a boy for striking me;** 24 **For if Cain is being avenged seven times, then Lamech will be avenged 77 times."** Seventy-seven times more hurt in return was now the accepted amount of getting even. If that amount was personal, then how much worse will it get throughout the next generations? This is why I say when people get involved in this endless eye for an eye lifestyle, they become the bottom feeders in society. They are always looking down to a greater baseness of vengeful fulfillment, rather than looking up to heaven for healing for their generational hurts.

If we want to get even with anything in life, we must put ourselves at the same starting line the Lord is standing on. If we start from the top and work the hurt and problem from the top where the Lord is ministering to our soul, we will have ammunition toward the temptation to lower ourselves to the lowest common denominator of street thug. Yes, there is always forgiveness when we finally turn back to the Lord, but hard to do when we have spent so much time living in past hurts and fantasies of revenge. Jesus uses a reference to put on His yoke. The picture is you are yoked or walking even with Him side-by-side, working out all the problems and hurts. As long as we stay yoked, we will be even with the Lord and that is a place to put our energies into getting even. Let us get close and personal with our Savior. That path leads to forgiveness and peace. May we all find it.

THE PAST HAS PASSED

Proverbs 4:26 Ponder the path of thy feet, and let all thy ways be established.

I was looking at some of my wife's old home-movies that my father-in-law had made in the mid 1950's. There was a sense of optimism in the actions of the people being filmed and excitement on the faces of everyone who were in these 8mm silent-home-made movies of family record. The future looked bright and seemed full of great and wonderful possibilities. I realized I was putting a nostalgic and positive spin on what I was looking at, because I knew the outcome of where most of these people were at today. I was looking at everything with my rose-colored-glasses and, most likely, I was mistaken at my own interpretation of everyone's life events. I had almost fallen into the trap of saying, "The good old days." The only thing good about the good old days is that they are gone. Phil. 3:13 **Brethren, I count not myself to have apprehended: but this one thing I do, forgetting those things which are behind, and reaching forth unto those things which are before 14 I press toward the mark for the prize of the high calling of God in Christ Jesus.**

Focusing on the past can paralyze us from moving toward the future God has planned toward our well-being. Luke 17:32 **Remember Lot's wife.** I am not saying do not look at old home-movies; as a matter of fact, please do, and you will have a fun time of belly laughter that will bring health to your souls. Prov. 17:22 **A merry heart does good like a medicine.** I am saying you cannot go back. What happened back then, was then, and this is now. Absentee fathers cannot bemoan the fact that they were not there to tuck in their children at bedtime. Runaway children cannot go back and enter their lost home-life today. Alcoholic mothers cannot go back and coo away all the hurts caused by drunkenness. All of these extremes messes can only be healed by the Balm of Gilead that Christ spreads across our hearts. None of us can go back to our past and fix the events that caused the state of our present day biology.

The question we must ask ourselves is, what do we do today? When will we stop using the excuses of the past to allow our present day misbehavior? When will we grow up? 1 Cor. 13:11 **When I was a child, I spake as a child, I understood as a child, I thought as a child: but when I became a man, I put away childish things.** Our church counseling rooms are busily occupied with bruised and sorrowful people who will not forgive their past, or are obsessed with returning to the past to try and accomplish a fix that is truly an impossible mission. Their daily song becomes Isa. 6:5-A **Then said I, Woe is me! for I am undone.** Sackcloth and ashes becomes their portion in life and the garment they wear. 2 Tim. 3:7 **Ever learning, and never able to come to the knowledge of the truth.**

Looking forward should be our position in Christ, but if we look back we might look at it in the way Og

Mandino quotes, "Whenever you make a mistake or get knocked down by life, don't look back at it too long. Mistakes are life's way of teaching you. Your capacity for occasional blunders is inseparable from your capacity to reach your goals. No one wins them all, and your failures, when they happen, are just part of your growth. Shake off your blunders. How will you know your limits without an occasional failure? Never quit. Your turn will come." The Lord would say it this way. Luke 9:62 **And Jesus said unto him, No man, having put his hand to the plough, and looking back, is fit for the kingdom of God.**

We read in chapter eleven in the book of Hebrews, a recorded list of the heroes of faith. They were not people who lingered long around their past shortcomings and failures. They went forward believing God, and that faith was accounted to them as righteousness. With the righteousness they had, they overcame incredible odds. We have a better covenant in Christ who has blessed us with His overcoming ability and grace. Let us move forward seeking Him first in all things and forgiving the past with the Lord's help. Matt. 6:33 **But seek ye first the kingdom of God, and his righteousness; and all these things shall be added unto you.**

THE MISERY OF REVENGE

Proverbs 20:22 Say not thou, I will recompense evil; but wait on the LORD, and he shall save thee.

A couple of blogs ago I wrote *Forgiving The Unforgivable.* I got a lot of feedback and conversations within my circle of friends, parishioners and family. One of the common statements amounted to the fact that there was a fear that the person who did the harm to the victim would get away with what they did if the victim forgave the bully. In so many words this was the injustice of it all. In one case I said, "If you do not forgive them, you will remain the miserable person you have become because of your stubbornness to hang on to the hurt. It is eating you alive." In this particular case the person who had done the hurting did not know they had done so. Who is in bondage here? Matt. 6:14 **For if ye forgive men their trespasses, your heavenly Father will also forgive you.** This whole notion of getting even does not work in a living and breathing environment. We change every day because of the indwelling of the Holy Spirit. Also, we are no longer the same people we were when we got hurt and the person who did the hurting is no longer the same person, for good or bad. If the terrible event happened more than seven years ago, the abuser and the victim no longer exist in body because every cell in their bodies have changed and regenerated. We are a whole new person according to our cells, yet the recollections of our hurt continue and live on fresh in our hearts. Why are they fresh? The enemy of our soul will not let us forget them until we forgive and hand judgement over to God. 1 Pet. 5:8 **Be sober, be vigilant; because your adversary the devil, as a roaring lion, walks about, seeking whom he may devour.** I'm not saying not to defend yourself in life. I'm saying getting even is God's job, not ours.

There is a saying, "He who goes to law for a sheep loses his cow." That is how they used to say, "Lawyers are real expensive, or you are going to pay way more for the satisfaction and justice you think you are owed." As the proverb says, "Say not thou, I will recompense evil." I will get even one day and then they will see how much they hurt me. Not true. They will not see anything if they are the self-absorbed people they were when they hurt you the first time.

The thing is, will you see what you have become when there is no joy in your heart because the revenge has no power? God will not take part in our unforgiveness or our vengefulness because God sent His son to forgive the world and not just ourselves. John 3:16 **For God so loved the world, that He gave His only begotten Son, that whosoever believes in Him should not perish, but have everlasting life.**

Someone wrote, "Unforgiveness is the single most popular poison that the enemy uses against God's people, and it is one of the deadliest poisons a person can take spiritually." I whole-heartily agree. The built-up desire for revenge and personal justice can lead to some serious sickness within people's lives. We were created in the image of God to extend grace, not fester and retain evil thoughts of revenge. Rom. 12:19 **Dearly**

beloved, avenge not yourselves, but rather give place unto wrath: for it is written, Vengeance is mine; I will repay, saith the Lord. Heb. 10:30 **For we know Him that hath said, Vengeance belongs unto me, I will recompense, saith the Lord. And again, The Lord shall judge his people.** 31 **It is a fearful thing to fall into the hands of the living God.** The older I get the more I realize it is a daily walk, because each day has enough battles without dragging the old offenses of the past into this day's battle zone. The devil's strategy of getting us to remember the hurts of the past and fret about the fears of the future leaves no place to live for Christ today. Matt. 6:34 **So don't worry about tomorrow, for tomorrow will bring its own worries. Today's trouble is enough for today.** Today is the day of salvation and today is the day to stop wanting a vengeful justice that will not satisfy, or in most cases, will never happen. Personal revenge becomes a complete waste of time. Again, who is in bondage here?

I heard a story of a woman who had been raped and beat-up in Central Park, New York City, while jogging in a secluded area. When she was released from the hospital, she was asked by reporters about her horrible assault. She stated that she had decided to forgive her attacker and leave the matter to the police. She said, "The man who did this to me owned my life for one day and he will never own another moment of my life. Therefore, I forgive and will go on to be healed." My thoughts were, what a graceful and powerful woman of incredible strength. I wondered if I could be so gracious and forgiving.

Then I thought, God can get to work on the heart of this predator who had brutally assaulted this woman. I ask you, "What do you think happened to him?" Heb. 10:31 **It is a fearful thing to fall into the hands of the living God.** Only God can administer true justice and apply vengeance for everyone. God wants us to hand vengeance over to Him. 1 Cor. 5:5 **To deliver such an one unto Satan for the destruction of the flesh, that the spirit may be saved in the day of the Lord Jesus.**

FORGIVING THE UNFORGIVABLE

Proverbs 20:20 Whoso curses his father or his mother, his lamp shall be put out in obscure darkness.

Forgiving those who have betrayed or harmed us is hard. Even harder is forgiving family members who have done the same. We read of a family betrayal that if it were done today would bring out every type of law enforcement, let alone televise all the emotional scars that would be carved on the person's soul. Joseph suffered this type of betrayal. Gen. 37:26 **And Judah said unto his brethren, What profit is it if we slay our brother, and conceal his blood** 27 **Come, and let us sell**

him to the Ishmaelites, and let not our hand be upon him; for he is our brother and our flesh. And his brethren were content. It says, "His brothers were content." This is hardheartedness. To be content with a decision not to murder a brother, but rather agree that selling their family member into slavery is a better option? This is all wrong. How did the family become so cold? Yet, after many years Joseph forgives his entire family. Gen. 45:4 **And Joseph said unto his brethren, Come near to me, I pray you. And they came near. And he said, I am Joseph your brother, whom ye sold into Egypt.** 15 **Moreover he kissed all his brethren, and wept upon them: and after that his brethren talked with him.**

My father was a sick and brutal man. I had a horrific childhood, but I have never used the events of that childhood as an excuse to become a criminal, addict or abusive. Were the opportunities available to become an addicted abusive criminal? Yes, but no thanks. Did I struggle with some of the shrapnel that lodged itself in my soul? Yes, but with time and the grace of my Lord Jesus I was delivered from its pain and crushing weight through forgiving my father. In 1996 I wrote the story called *I'm telling on you Doug.* These are memories of when I was five years old. This next paragraph is an except from that story describing the abuse that was suffered by myself and my mother, but most important, the eventual forgiveness of the whole time.

Down came his hand with a slap, then up flew the fist with a punch and a smothered sound that accompanies the impact of the blow. The rage in his voice mingled with the choreography of two people entangled in a blur of each other's movements. Blood stains are creating new patterns on the dress that my mother is wearing, and smearing the floor in the area of this dance of violence. I am paralyzed with fear and apprehension, because as I see the blood flowing from my mother's beaten face I can no longer look up at the longing expression of helplessness in her eyes. I feel incapacitated, because I am not able to help deliver her from this present anguish. I am slipping into myself as my eyes cannot look beyond the blood stained waistline of her dress, because beyond this point I cannot understand or carry this hideous image in my psyche. The fabrics of our lives are knitted with screaming, arguing, bludgeon backhands, and the acrimonious intent of our destruction.

Will this ever end?

This is a small part of a large story that we suffered fifty-six years ago. I give testimony that my mother and I are healed and living a blessed life. My mother is now married to a good man of God who loves her dearly, and I am walking in the peace and joy of the power of forgiveness. Matt. 5:44 **But I say unto you, Love your enemies, bless them that curse you, do good to them that hate you, and pray for them which despitefully use you, and persecute you.** Forgiving the unforgivable is what Christ did for each one of us. His grace was extended to me so that I could extend it to my father who truly needed all of our Lord's grace and forgiveness. When you forgive the unforgivable, you are allowing all the bondage's and family curses to be broken and repeated no more. My family has never felt an angry backhand against their faces. I sow peace into my next generation by forgiving my past. It is time to man-up and get healed, saints. Stand tall, put your shoulders back and shout it out loud,"I forgive you completely in Christ." Luke 23:34-A **Then said Jesus, Father, forgive them; for they know not what they do.**

BECAUSE I'M FORGIVEN

Proverbs 25:21 If thine enemy be hungry, give him bread to eat; and if he be thirsty, give him water to drink.

Years ago when I was ministering in Australia an elderly missionary said to me, "Think of the person you love the least and that is the most amount of love you have for the Lord." How do we know if the love of Christ has really changed our hearts? When we start praying and blessing our enemies and the people who have abused us. Matt. 5:44 **But I say unto you, Love your enemies, bless them that curse you, do good to them that hate you, and**

pray for them which despitefully use you, and persecute you.

Many of us can think of people who have hurt us, impacting our hearts and attitudes, with negative choices or positive ones depending how we process the hurt. My father was a brutal man and hurt me severely, but one day God asked me to forgive him. This took a lot of time and heartfelt growing; however, with the help of the Holy Spirit eventually I was free from all the memories and effects of my father's abuse toward me. Mark 11:25 **And when ye stand praying, forgive, if ye have ought against any: that your Father also which is in heaven may forgive you your trespasses.** I was honestly able to pray for my dad's salvation and restoration toward all our family members. Did this erase the evil actions toward me that were done? No, but by faith I chose to cancel the debt that was owed me the same way the Lord Jesus canceled my debt owed God. Free at last from all past sins and hurts. It is the only way to be set free from all the horrors that were unjustly inflicted on us who have been victimised by the bullies in life. Did Jesus deserve what happened to Him at the cross? I am sure you can answer that yourselves.

Many of us want the forgiveness of God for ourselves and the judgement of God for those who have harmed us. The truth is that we have all fallen short of God's perfection, but by His grace and forgiveness His love will heal us. Rom. 5:8 **But God commended His love toward us, in that, while we were yet sinners, Christ died for us.** We were saved by grace, (God's unmerited favour) then we were filled with His grace (God's ability in us) so that we would extend grace (unmerited favour) to others. That is how we are going to be able to forgive those who have trespassed against us.

There is a story of a wicked servant who had been forgiven a great debt owed a king. The debt became impossible for the servant to pay it back in full, but the king out of his mercy forgave the debt that was owed him. However, when the wicked servant found someone who owed him a small amount he would not extend the same mercy that was given to himself. Matt. 18:32 **Then his lord, after that he had called him, said unto him, O thou wicked servant, I forgave thee all that debt, because thou desired me:** 33 **Should not thou also have had compassion on thy fellow servant, even as I had pity on thee?** 35 **So likewise shall my heavenly Father do**

also unto you, if ye from your hearts forgive not every one his brother their trespasses.

This is how the kingdom of God works when it comes to forgiveness, and if we are in His kingdom then that is how we must extend forgiveness. The wicked servant owed a debt he could not pay, but the king forgave his debt. The wicked servant was owed a debt that could be eventually paid, but would not extend the same mercy freely offered to himself. In the same way we owed God an eternal debt that we could not pay, but God in His mercy and grace forgave our debt completely; therefore, we should also forgive the debts owed us by the people who also have access to the same forgiveness that was freely given to us.

Is it easy to extend a merciful heart to someone who has violated our lives?

No, it is not easy, but it is necessary in order for us to move forward and be an overcomer in Christ. This is something we will have to bring to the Lord in prayer and work throughout our Christian lives, but it will be worth it in the end. Rev. 12:11 **And they overcame him by the blood of the Lamb, and by the word of their testimony; and they loved not their lives unto the death.**

FORGIVING THE PAST

Proverbs 10:32 The lips of the righteous know what is acceptable: but the mouth of the wicked speaks frowardness.

I read this sentence in a news article. "I never felt really healthy. The best I could feel was - not sick." I understood what she was saying because I was wondering the same thing about my own life during the past Christmas holidays. I had been explaining these same feelings to my son and we pondered and wondered if I would ever rise above - not being sick. I am happy to say that I did come through to a healthier place and still progressing onward. I did it with a lot of prayer and seeking God. Psalm 127:1 **Except the LORD build the house, they labour in vain that build it: except the LORD keep the city, the watchman wakes but in vain.** Healthy living and being proactive in one's health choices in order to rise above the norm is far better than just being on the verge of sickness and disease, as in borderline diabetics, recovering alcoholics, first stages of dementia and so on. That place of living is not a healthy place to be in, unless you are already headed to health from that place of borderline sickness.

Some of the people who struggle with forgiving their past are experiencing the same thing as the people who are just not sick. They have gone through the motions of forgiving the ones who have hurt them, but experience no real freedom. They have forgiven in a way that seems to work until the memory or encounter with that person or situation explodes again. Forgiving under our own terms with strings attached will continue to bind us up. Why does God admonish us to forgive everyone and the part they played in our past? So that we may go forward without hindrances! That is it in its simplicity. Psalm 103:4 **But with you there is forgiveness, so that we can, with reverence, serve you.** Living in a place with an unforgiving heart will hinder our lives in all that we do. Forgiving the hurtful events from our past will set us free for today and the future. However, the forgiveness we offer must be a choice of forgiving completely. Mark 11:26 **But if ye do not forgive, neither will your Father which is in heaven forgive your trespasses.**

Deep down we all know it is the right

thing to do because we have all felt the joy of being forgiven. Psalm 32:1 **How joyful is the one whose transgression is forgiven, whose sin is covered!** We have all felt the freedom forgiveness gives us when we have been forgiven and pardoned for something of great significance. How many siblings need to forgive each other for the scars encountered while growing up in a volatile and brutal family? How many divorced people need to forgive their deplorable spouse for the unfaithfulness and utter feelings of being betrayed to the core of their hearts? We all know of unspeakable things that have been done to others that defy reason and human understanding, yet God asks us to forgive all the sins and memories of the past. As Derek Prince says, "Forgiving is not an emotion, it's a decision." We choose to obey God by forgiving the past.

What courage this action takes in the life of the believer in Christ. The fortitude of walking forward and saying, "I forgive you completely," leaves many speechless because of the great burden of debt lifted from the accused shoulders. What most people do not realize is that the one forgiving is the one who gets set free the most because this graceful action cuts all ties of misunderstood justice. They are no longer just not sick, but walking healthy in the love and power of the Holy Spirit. They no longer wear the coat of blame, excuses and rationalization that they have come to rely upon for their lack of growth in the Kingdom of God. In forgiving completely, these brave souls have removed the vestment of hurt and put on the robe of righteous strength and walk purposefully in the peace that passes all understanding. Phil. 4:7 **And the peace of God, which passes all understanding, shall keep your hearts and minds through Christ Jesus.**

Prov. 10:32 **The lips of the righteous know what is acceptable: but the mouth of the wicked speaks frowardness.** When we say, "I forgive you completely," our lips of righteousness know it is the right thing to say. When we do not forgive completely, our conversation will prove our choice by the duplicity being voiced from our soul. As we get older in life and mature in our walk with Christ, it is no longer good enough to be just not sick. We need to walk in the health of the power of the grace of God and be the righteous witnesses Christ has made us to be. My sins were many and Christ forgave me completely. I can only say,

"Lord, teach my lips to speak acceptable words of forgiveness and peace to all who have hurt me and are in need of your merciful salvation as I have been blessed to walk in." Thank you Lord.

THERE ARE ENEMIES

Proverbs 16:7 When a man's ways please the LORD, He makes even his enemies to be at peace with him.

My pride is ruining my testimony because I want the grace of God in my life, but I want God's judgment on my enemies lives without mercy. Well saints, this pride will not do. In order for my enemies to be at peace with me, I must please the Lord. God's first order of faith is in Him, and second that I love my neighbours and my enemies' as myself. Mark 12:30 **And thou shalt love the Lord thy God with all thy heart, and with all thy soul, and with all thy mind, and with all thy**

strength: this is the first commandment. 31 **And the second is like, namely this, Thou shalt love thy neighbour as thyself. There is none other commandment greater than these.** Luke 6:27 **But I say unto you which hear, Love your enemies, do good to them which hate you.**
Choices in life are most often simple, but not always easy to live out.

We read in the book of Genesis the story of Joseph who was betrayed by his brothers because of jealousy. After years of slavery and imprisonment, Joseph emerges as second-in-command only to Pharaoh himself. Joseph's brothers come to Egypt to buy food because of a great famine in the land. Now they must deal with Joseph who is now in a position of great power and can exact revenge. However, Joseph forgives his brothers. Gen. 45:4 **And Joseph said**

unto his brethren, Come near to me, I pray you. And they came near. And he said, I am Joseph your brother, whom ye sold into Egypt. 5 **Now therefore be not grieved, nor angry with yourselves, that ye sold me hither: for God did send me before you to preserve life.** There was a lot for Joseph to forgive here; yet he could see that it was God who had directed his life and turned everything to the good for Joseph personally. He also preserved a nation from starvation. God made his enemies to be at peace with him and better yet, Joseph was also at peace with his enemies who were now restored brothers.

Truly the Psalmist says it right in Psalm 23:5 **Thou preparest a table before me in the presence of mine enemies: thou anointest my head with oil; my cup runs over.** This is our portion of a full cup when we are walking in a way that pleases the Lord. We will live in peace even though there are enemies in our lives, whether they are spiritual or natural enemies. Deut. 28:7 **The LORD shall cause thine enemies that rise up against thee to be smitten before thy face: they shall come out against thee one way, and flee before thee seven ways.** This does not mean we will never encounter problems or demonic attacks, but it means we will have the confidence in our God who will help us with the battle these protagonists bring. Deut. 20:4 **For the LORD your God is He that goes with you, to fight for you against your enemies, to save you.** The fact that we are believing, by faith, that God is our ever-present-help is pleasing to God and He will go to war and fight the enemies of our lives. God will rebuke

the devourer for our sakes and restore what was taken from us. 2 Kings 17:39 **But the LORD your God ye shall fear; and he shall deliver you out of the hand of all your enemies.**
The blessing of this incredible benefit from God is that we can count on the Lord to take this fight of the destruction of our enemies to the very end. Death is the last enemy we will contend with in our lifetime. 1 Cor. 15:26 **The last enemy that shall be destroyed is death.** The finished work of the cross of Jesus Christ has consumed our eternal death and all the fears that come with it. The Psalmist says that we will be guided even unto death. Psalm 48:14 **For this God is our God for ever and ever: He will be our guide even unto death.** We now have victory over death and will be guided through this process that can overwhelm us and cause fearful

thoughts from this last enemy. The Lord encourages us not to fear this enemy because He has overcome death for us. 1 Cor. 15:55 **O death, where is thy sting? O grave, where is thy victory?** When a man's ways please the LORD, He makes even his enemies to be at peace with him. What an amazing salvation we have that death, our last enemy, has been defeated by the cross and blood of our Lord and Savior Jesus Christ. Rev. 1:8 **I am he that lives, and was dead; and, behold, I am alive for evermore, Amen; and have the keys of hell and of death.**

Lord, we ask in Jesus name, that you continue to remind us of your powerful work that was done in our hearts and in our lives. Lord, you have saved us from the deceptions of the enemy. You, LORD, alone have defeated all our enemies - including death - and we are grateful. Amen

DELIVERED FROM GUILT AND SHAME

Proverbs 13:18 Poverty and shame shall be to him that refuses instruction: but he that regards reproof shall be honoured.

We have all known the unsettling sensation of guilt and shame when we know we've done something wrong. But, oh, the blessing of the Lord's forgiveness through the blood of Christ that takes away our sins and the resulting shame that plagued our lives. When you think of it, what an amazing power the blood has to be able to bring real peace and joy to a once heavy heart because of sin. There is nothing that can be compared to God's awesome power, ability and willingness to clear and clean a shame-ridden conscience from the guilt of a heavy heart. God asks us to choose His life-giving gift. He leaves it up to us whether we will have a clear conscience or carry the burden of shame. Deut. 30:19 **I call heaven and earth to record this day against you, that I have set before you life and death, blessing and cursing: therefore choose life, that both thou and thy seed may live.**

Guilt and shame can paralyze a person's spirit to the point of giving up on life. Judas Iscariot, who had betrayed Jesus, tried to turn things around after he realized what he had done to the Lord. Matt. 27:3 **When Judas, who had betrayed him, realized that Jesus had been condemned to die, he was filled with remorse. So he took the thirty pieces of silver back to the**

leading priests and the elders. Here is the irony for Judas. He went to the priest of the day to try to reverse the cause of his sin, but there was no real help for him. The priests were not interested in the soul of a sinner, unlike the love that Christ has for the sinner. The priests were only interested in the perks of the office of the priesthood. Judas looked for forgiveness of sin and the removal of the guilt it caused, but there was no redemption found in his present system. Matt. 27:4 "**I have sinned," he declared, "for I have betrayed an innocent man." "What do we care?" they retorted. "That's your problem."** Ouch! What an answer from the spiritual leaders of the day. The detrimental action that Judas took was the result of the deep and overwhelming depression, guilt and shame that resulted from the sin. Matt.

27:5 **So Judas threw the money into the temple and left. Then he went away and hanged himself.**

The Proverb says that poverty and shame shall be to him that refuses instruction. Life is hard enough without being in a state of poverty. However, when the poverty and shame is of our own doing it can truly be remorseful. Thank God there is grace and a way out of a shameful and poverty-stricken situation. The word of God says in Prov. 19:20 **Get all the advice and instruction you can, so you will be wise the rest of your life.** When you have wisdom because you submitted to God's instruction, you will come out of poverty and the shame of the past events will be lifted from your soul because you will be walking with the Lord who is your wisdom and the Savior of your soul. Why is it so important to come out from under the bondage of guilt and shame? It sets us free to believe the restoration power of God in our lives. When we are delivered from guilt and shame through the blood of Jesus Christ, it positions us to live our lives in a place of receiving the blessing of the Lord. Restoration becomes one of our blessings.

God said He would restore our health. Jer. 30:17-**A For I will restore health unto thee, and I will heal thee of thy wounds, saith the LORD**. The word of God also says that God would restore our soul. Psalm 23:3 **He restores my soul: he leads me in the paths of righteousness for his name's sake**. With joy, the Lord will restore what was stolen from us over the years of our life. Joel 2:25 **And I will restore to you the years that the locust hath eaten, the cankerworm, and the**

caterpiller, and the palmerworm, my great army which I sent among you. Oh, yes Lord, deliver us from shame and guilt that we may walk in the abundant favor that you have for each one of us who loves you and delight in your love for us. Teach us, Lord God, to love your instruction and respond to it when we hear it. Help us to be Christians of honor. Amen!

INDEX OF FEATURED PROVERBS

ABOUT THE AUTHOUR

I currently live in the beautiful city of Kelowna, British Columbia. It was during an Okanagan Valley summer of 1979 Jesus Christ, through faith, became my Lord and Savior. At that time I was struggling with being functionally illiterate. I was transferred into an English school from a French school at the beginning of grade five; therefore, I missed all the fundamental rules of grammar and diction for reading and writing English.

In 1980 while attending Commonwealth Bible College in Katoomba, New South Wales, Australia, I miraculously started to understand how to read and write. Through prayer and faith God gave me the gift to memorise and remember scripture in vast amounts. Out of this blessing my ability to read and write grew rapidly to the point where I could teach the Word of God at a college learning level.

After living in Australia for six years working and ministering in different capacities of Christian ministry, I returned to Canada. Since that time I have been assisting at the Kelowna Christian Center Society.

For my entire adult life I have been employed as a sales rep for a security company and also offering my ministry services to the body of Christ. The blessing of living in this time of great possibilities through all the technologies available to us is truly amazing. The blog, Sir Norm's Proverbial Comment, is one of the tools I am using to reach out and be a blessing.

This book is a collection of blogs written for Christians who are looking for help and inspiration to keep walking strong in their faith. I love reading the Proverbs as there is a proverb that can answer most events or situations that occur in life. By writing the blog and now this book, it is my hope that the subjects written about would aid every individual to live righteously and well in this day and age.

CONNECT WITH NORM

Norm's Blog "Sir Norm's Proverbial Comment" can be found online in English, French and Spanish. Your comments on any of the hundreds of blog posts are appreciated.

Sir Norm's Proverbial Comment:
https://sirnorm1.blogspot.ca/

Commentaire Proverbial de Sir Norm:
https://sirnorm.blogspot.ca/

Comentario Proverbial de Sir Norm:
https://sirnorm-1.blogspot.ca/

89471894R00191

Made in the USA
San Bernardino, CA
25 September 2018